BABY &
KIDSPACE
IDEA BOOK

BABY & KIDSPACE
IDEA BOOK

Wendy A. Jordan and Suzonne Stirling

The Taunton Press

The Taunton Press
Inspiration for hands-on living®

The Taunton Press, Inc., 63 South Main Street, PO Box 5506,
Newtown, CT 06470-5506
e-mail: tp@taunton.com

ILLUSTRATORS: Christine Erickson and Martha Garstang Hill
COVER PHOTOGRAPHERS: Front cover: (top row, left to right) ©Wendell T. Webber,
©Robert Mauer Photography, ©Mark Samu/Samu Studios, ©Stephen Smith Images;
(bottom row, left to right) courtesy The Warm Biscuit Bedding Company, ©Feinknopt
Photography, ©Lisa Romerein, ©Lisa Romerein.
Back cover: (top photo) ©Sharon Haege, Brink House Creative; (bottom row, left to
right) ©Chun Y Lai, ©Wendell T. Webber, ©Chipper Hatter, ©Wendell T. Webber.

Library of Congress Cataloging-in-Publication Data

Jordan, Wendy Adler, 1946-
  Baby & kidspace idea book / Wendy A. Jordan and Suzonne Stirling.
     p. cm.
  ISBN-13: 978-1-56158-860-2
  ISBN-10: 1-56158-860-1
  1. Children's rooms. 2. Interior decoration. I. Title: Baby and kidspace idea book. II.
Stirling, Suzonne. III. Title.
  NK2117.C4J665 2006
   747.7'7083--dc22
                                    2005029671

Printed in Singapore
10 9 8 7 6 5 4 3 2 1

Contents

Chapter 3
Bedrooms for Kids ▪ 94

Contents *(continued)*

Chapter 4
Places to Play, Places to Study · 160

Introduction

BABYSPACE IDEA BOOK

The moment you cross the threshold of your home with a new baby, life as you know it is forever transformed: Your emotional world expands, you realize how much you're capable of with little sleep, and you find out just how much you have to learn. If it's your first child, this humbling experience is even more profound.

Your home and lifestyle go through a similar transition, as you're forced to examine your surroundings through a

child's eyes, learning to baby proof as you go and swapping out an adults-only lifestyle for one that accommodates the little one in your life. And then there's the space factor, as mountains of baby gear suddenly show up in your cozy home once meant for two.

That's where this book comes in. It's filled with ideas to help make the transition a more comfortable one. There's no "one size fits all" approach here, but rather an understanding of the myriad challenges that new parents face, from creating a nursery to sharing their bedroom with an infant.

Like children, *Babyspace Idea Book* doesn't stop at infancy. It moves on to toddlers' rooms, with an emphasis on long-term design for parents living in today's overly busy world. The book also examines play spaces, honoring this important element of a child's development with cleverly designed rooms and hideaways that fully embrace the kids who create magic there. Then there's the rest of the house, where the focus is on making it a home for everyone, children and adults alike.

This book also tackles organizational challenges throughout the home, an important aspect of a pleasant and comfortable environment. Again, there's no

single solution presented here, but rather a variety of ideas that anyone can incorporate into their existing floor plan.

Use *Babyspace Idea Book* to help you navigate your new lifestyle, inspire creative thought, develop long-term design strategies, and problem-solve. More important, use it as a foundation for your own unique style and a guide for bringing personal contributions to your home.

Welcome to a new world!

—Suzonne Stirling

NEW KIDSPACE IDEA BOOK

Kids' rooms are in a class by themselves. Other parts of the house may be designed with a certain reserve, but the most appealing spaces for children are those that are created with abandon and joy. Of course, there are implicit rewards in crafting an environment for children. We have the pleasure of shaping a setting that fosters both fun and learning, a place where kids can thrive and grow. And besides, we're all young at heart; designing rooms for kids draws on our own playfulness and youthful spirit.

I was impressed by that "fun factor" in kids' room designs when I collected ideas for the original *Kidspace Idea Book*. I'm even more impressed by it now. The first

book offered hundreds of excellent designs from around the country and beyond, and I was happy to learn that designers and homeowners alike found much inspiration in those pages. It was particularly gratifying to know that the book was used exactly as we had intended —as a source of ideas to build on and personalize rather than simply reproduce.

I began researching kidspaces again and discovered a whole new generation of wonderful designs, all of them fresh and vibrant. Those new designs are presented in this book. Some are big ideas— dream rooms, you might say. They are here to inspire, not intimidate. In fact, I've made a point of zeroing in on the

specific ideas contained in these rooms so that you can apply them as a package or make à la carte selections. In either case, you can interpret the ideas as you wish and make them your own.

Other ideas are simpler but just as creative. I've highlighted many economical ideas, easy-to-implement techniques, and shortcuts to great designs. There is something for everyone in these pages: designs for kids of all ages; projects for do-it-yourselfers as well as those that may be best handled by professionals; approaches for whole rooms as well as room areas and components; off-the-shelf as well as custom solutions; clever built-ins as well as room-making accessories.

All the pieces are here. With a touch of your own imaginative spark you can combine them to create kidspaces just right for your needs.

—Wendy Jordan

1

Nurseries

Long before you decide on your baby's name, you will probably start planning her nursery. Perhaps you already have an extra room earmarked, complete with a mental image of the perfect nursery. Or you may be like most of us, trying to figure out how to make room for a new baby and feeling overwhelmed by furniture and color choices and all those baby names! So where do you begin?

The best way to get to know a room is to spend some time there. Judge the quality of light in the room, how the temperature relates to the rest of the house, and any awkward corners or areas of the room that need to be considered.

Once you've gotten a feel for the room, it's time to move on to choosing furniture. While practicality and safety should have top priority, you should also remember that creating a nursery isn't just a practical experience; you're preparing your heart and home for a momentous transition.

Enjoy the process. Open your mind to fresh ideas and new perspectives (good parenting advice, as well). Don't be afraid of color, feel free to shake things up, and welcome new life into your home.

◄ TEXTURE AND GENTLY COLORED ACCENTS keep a mostly white interior from feeling stark or sterile, as shown by this classic nursery. Detailed trim gives the room depth and prevents woodwork from blending in with the wallpaper, while subtle patterns in the rug add visual interest to the floor.

Starting with the Basics

NO MATTER WHAT THE CIRCUMSTANCES, most nurseries have four basic items: a crib, a changing table, a nursing chair, and some type of storage. These should be hardworking, well-made pieces. But besides being practical, each element can function as a building block for additional design. Find a piece of furniture you love and an entire room can be created around it.

Ultimately, your goal in designing a nursery is to create a functional, efficient space that feels warm and welcoming for your baby. It should also be a room *you* feel comfortable in. After all, a nursery is as much a parent's home in the first year as it is the baby's, perhaps more so.

So keep it simple. Keep it basic. But definitely let it reflect who you are and what you love.

▲ INVESTING IN A COMFORTABLE ROCKING CHAIR may seem like a luxury, but it quickly becomes a necessity as late-night feedings take their toll on a weary parent. A plain storage cube with a painted interior becomes a charming decorative element as well as an impromptu tabletop.

▼ AN ALL-WHITE CRIB AND ACCESSORIES are soothing rather than bland, with a mix of textures and subtle color variations to engage the senses. The soft yellow of the wall enhances the natural light streaming into the room, giving it a warm, golden glow.

▲ STORAGE BECOMES DECORATIVE, not merely utilitarian, with an eclectic assortment of containers stashed inside a simple wardrobe. Cheerful lined shelves and washable basket liners add charm and color, in addition to being useful.

▲ THIS SIMPLE CHANGING TABLE comes with a removable cushioned pad. When baby gets older the pad can be removed and the piece used for toy storage. Wicker baskets keep clutter at bay and provide textural detail to a basic setup.

▲ PARING DOWN TO BASICS is a natural choice for enhancing the minimalist design aesthetic favored by these urban parents. The crib, with its traditional yet clean styling, easily harmonizes with adult furnishings and fixtures while the nursing chair, though modern in feel, curves around the body for comfort.

▲ THE CRIB TAKES CENTER STAGE in this nursery with its vivid bedding and prominent architectural design. A drop-latch side rail makes it easy for parents to reach inside of the crib, and the broad molding on both headboard and footboard prevents baby's clothing from getting caught.

▶ SUBSTANTIAL FURNITURE warms up the nursery and doesn't require much accessorizing. The pieces shown here are also good investments as the dresser can be used throughout childhood, while the crib will easily convert to a toddler bed in the future.

Safety Basics

CREATING A HAZARD-FREE ENVIRONMENT should be a top priority. Planning your nursery with safety in mind will save time, money, and unnecessary stress later in the process.

- Keep a working smoke and carbon monoxide detector in or near the nursery.
- Cover all electrical outlets.
- Avoid floor-length curtains or drapes; a crawling baby can easily pull them down.
- Blinds with long cords are a strangulation risk. Install a cleat or hook high up on the window frame and loop cords around it, completely out of baby's reach.
- Gather and secure any electrical cords with a twist-tie.
- Install window guards on windows and make sure latches are secure.
- Make sure heavy toy boxes have safety hinges on the top.
- Avoid floor lamps, which are easily knocked over.
- Install radiator guards.

▲ THIS RADIATOR COVER PROVIDES SAFETY while also serving as a decorative element that enhances the setting. The wide top can be used for extra storage.

CRIB SAFETY

- Use a crib with slats no more than 2³⁄₈ in. apart.
- Avoid cribs with cutouts in the headboards or footboards.
- Measure to be sure the top of the railing is at least 26 in. above the mattress.
- Beware of elevated corner posts on a crib; baby's clothing can get caught on them.
- Avoid cribs with easily released drop-side latches. Look for latches that require two distinct actions or a minimum force of 10 pounds with one action to release them.
- Make sure the mattress fits snugly in the frame.
- Keep pillows, comforters, quilts, and stuffed toys out of the crib. Remove the bumper once baby is able to pull himself to a standing position to prevent it from being used as a stepping stone.
- Never place a crib directly against a window; the sun is too strong for delicate skin, and baby may climb onto the windowsill.

CHANGING TABLE SAFETY

- Purchase a table with a flat, wide surface to easily accommodate a growing infant; high side rails offer extra protection.
- Storage space is important. You'll need to keep one hand on your baby at all times; everything you need should be well within reach.
- You'll need a padded surface for the top of the changing table. Choose a thick, contoured, waterproof pad, preferably with a safety strap.
- Protect your back; purchase a table that's a comfortable height for you.
- A good table will be stable when shaken; if not, bolt it to the wall.

Designing with Color

GONE ARE THE DAYS WHEN PARENTS SIMPLY PAINTED A ROOM pink or blue and called it quits. Today, color choices abound and parents are designing with an eye on the future. A pastel pink room can feel dated quickly, but take it up a few notches and you've got a color you can live with well beyond baby's first year.

Parents are also getting away from gender-specific colors and playing with strong, happy palettes that simply make kids feel joyful. It's a new, bright, colorful world and it's easy to get in on the fun. A couple of coats of paint and you've got a fresh makeover and a new outlook.

Another plus: More color allows you to get away with less accessorizing. And that's good for your budget!

▲ SMALL, SURPRISING DOSES OF COLOR can bring a neutral room to life. If vibrant wall color feels like too much of a commitment, pepper the nursery with lively accessories (like this switch-plate) that unify the room and provide stimulating focal points.

▶ A NEUTRAL, SUNNY YELLOW makes this room amenable to either sex and to a range of ages. A white crib keeps the look modern and fresh, while clever accents, like the shelf with hooks, message in letters above, and bright mobile, personalize the space.

▲ BOLD TONES GIVE THIS PAINT STAYING POWER, suitable far beyond infancy. The warm, bright pink provides an exuberant foundation with a decidedly feminine air. Details in the bedding and accents in the graceful furniture and accessories keep color center stage.

RETHINKING PASTELS

▲ A SUCCESSFUL MIX of powerful color and strong graphic prints create a joyful nursery with a fresh, modern punch. Classic white furniture, softly colored bedding, and neutral flooring keep the combination exciting, not jarring.

▶ PALE PINK BEDDING mellows the bright orange of the walls and calms baby for sleeping. A mix of polka dots and stripes are fun, yet feminine when expressed in a soft palette. A ruffled bed skirt and blanket add a flirty touch.

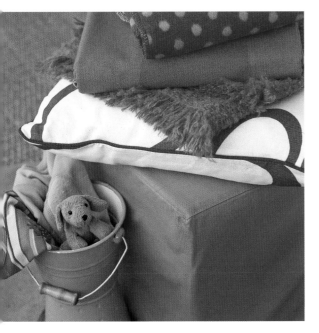

▲ MODERN GRAPHICS PAIRED WITH CLASSIC POLKA DOTS make a child-friendly statement in this nursery with its bold color scheme. Durable, crisp accents, such as the canvas ottoman and pillow, get softened by downy blankets, keeping the look warm and inviting rather than harsh.

◄ THINK OUTSIDE THE BOX when selecting paint colors for a nursery. Unexpected, saturated colors offer vibrancy and decorating longevity.

Improving Your Outlook

"THE PSYCHOLOGY BEHIND COLOR IS INCREDIBLY PERSONAL," says Barbara Richardson, color expert and director of color marketing for ICI Paints, maker of the Glidden® brand. "Adults have lifetime experiences they filter their perception of a color through. Their preferences come from strong emotional associations with the past, positive or negative experiences."

This is helpful to remember when you and your spouse simply can't agree on what color to paint the nursery. Delving beyond the personal, however, basic color psychology can help you create a room that's in harmony with your needs.

Red: Stimulates the appetite, heart rate, and breathing. Can make babies feel anxious, so it's better used as an accent color.

Orange: Associated with warmth and contentment; it's a nurturing color.

Yellow: Enhances concentration and stimulates learning, but it may make a baby cry more. It's the most eye-fatiguing color there is; if you're using it in a nursery, go softer rather than brighter.

Blue: Causes the opposite reaction as red. Relaxes the nervous system and has a tranquilizing effect, always helpful in a bedroom.

Pink: Calming; acts as a tranquilizer.

Green: The easiest color on the eye, it has a neutral effect on the nervous system; a serene, refreshing color.

White: Makes a room feel lighter and cooler.

▲ A FRESH APPROACH TO A TRADITIONAL COLOR gives this room a contemporary yet serene feel. Repeating the wall color in details throughout the room creates a feeling of cohesion, even with disparate furniture. An infusion of lime adds contrast and vibrancy.

▲ WITH ITS HUES OF LIME AND TURQUOISE, this nursery feels inspired by nature. Nontraditional baby elements such as this bamboo ladder, pressed into service as a repository for blankets, reinforce the idea. The color scheme is further echoed in a swatch of fabric that's become art thanks to a simple frame.

▲ AN OLD DRESSER benefits from a fresh coat of paint and contrasting knobs that pick up the hue from the walls. While currently doing double duty as a changing table, it's a solid transitional piece that will continue to be useful after baby is out of diapers.

▲ A STRONG, MODERN LAMP gets softened with stripes of aqua that bring it in line with the rest of the decor. It's an easy, do-it-yourself fix. Start with a basic opaque shade and use oil-based paint and masking tape to create your own complementary color accents.

COLOR THERAPY

Problem Solving with Paint

NOT A LOT OF LIGHT IN THE ROOM? Use a warm color like yellow or gold. Does the nursery get intense light? Use cool or darker colors to manage some of that intensity.

Drawn towards a particularly strong color but don't want it on every wall? Consider a neutral paint for three of the walls and ceiling. Then paint one feature wall with the strong color. Later, if you tire of it, it's easy to repaint.

Looking to create a calming atmosphere? Paint the room in a single color. Adding another color, particularly a complementary one, creates more energy, so this might be a better choice for a playroom.

WALL TREATMENTS

▶ PALE PINK WALLS BECOME positively dreamy with the addition of floating bubbles painted over the basic wall color—an effect suitable for a baby but fully appreciated once she has grown a bit. This nursery furniture is adaptable for an infant or toddler, making it a good investment.

▲ NOT YOUR TRADITIONAL BABY PATTERN, this wallpaper marries a sophisticated stripe with a classic color scheme. The result is soft and ethereal, needing only ribbons and polka-dotted bedding to add a playful, youthful touch.

▶ CLASSIC RICKRACK ON THE BED SKIRT becomes a playful design element for this wall. Achieved with three colors of paint, it pairs beautifully with the vintage-style floral print of the linens, an effect both classic and fresh.

▲ A WHIMSICAL SCENE from a nursery rhyme was painted on this bedroom wall, becoming a strong decorative element. Supplemental storage is offered on the shelf, which blends seamlessly with the mural, creating a compelling focal point over the dresser.

◄ IN LIEU OF PAINTING OR WALLPAPERING, a moveable mural gives baby something to be stimulated by and delineates the nursery area in a shared room. A large canvas covered with fabric would work just as effectively as this painted canvas.

◄ THIS FRIENDLY CATERPILLAR
was painted close to the floor,
where it will entertain the baby
when he is playing on the rug.
A stencil, decal, or wallpaper
cutout would work just as well
if your artistic skills are shaky.

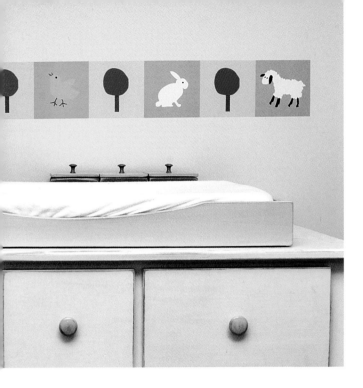

A STRIP OF ANIMAL IMAGES gives the baby something bright and intriguing to look at while she is on the changing table. Placed low on the wall so she can see it clearly, this peel-and-stick graphic can easily be moved or replaced.

◄ ► EVEN A ROOM WITH VERY FEW WINDOWS can be transformed into a sunny nursery. The soft glow of this basement room was achieved with rag-washed interior latex paint diluted with water. A few farmyard friends were added, as well as a topcoat of glaze that makes the walls washable.

Choosing Décor

ONCE UPON A TIME, designing a nursery was easy. Choices were limited. You started with pink, blue, or yellow. Maybe a lavender or mint green. Then you chose the bedding and baby accessories that fit conveniently into those color schemes, a ruffle for decoration, perhaps a stripe. One-stop shopping.

But parents slowly began to change the market, asking for products that were more stylish and appropriate for their home. This has resulted in color combinations that are more exciting, more sophisticated. Fabric patterns are fresh and fun, often without a baby motif. Furniture choices have expanded to include more streamlined and design-conscious pieces—an approach that gives the modern nursery longevity, making it appealing for older children as well.

Of course, you can still find traditional if that's what your heart desires. But it's also wonderful to have the option of mixing contemporary with traditional, of incorporating an eclectic mix that's a reflection of your personal aesthetic to create a room that truly embraces a new member of the family.

▲ A VINTAGE-STYLE CRIB with a sheer canopy is offset by fresh, modern floral bedding in a classic color scheme of pink and green. The subtle diamond pattern on the crib skirt adds visual interest to the floral bumper, a departure from the usual bedding sold in matching prints.

▶ CONTEMPORARY OPTIONS in furniture and bedding have expanded for style-conscious parents, as exemplified by this nursery with its nontraditional color palette and mixture of sophisticated and childlike elements. The tailored bedding feels clean and fresh, not babyish or cloying, a design choice that holds up over time.

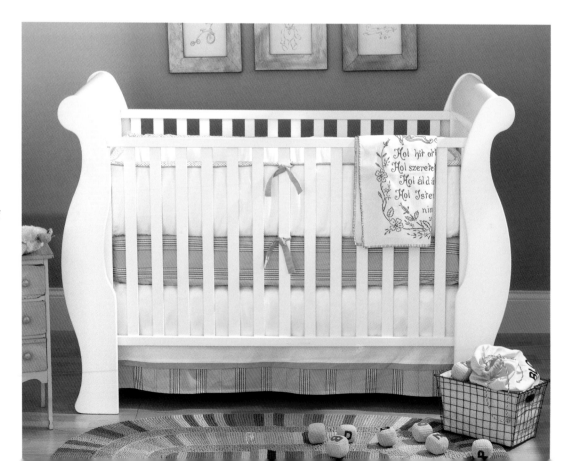

Feathering the Nest

THE CRIB IS MORE IMPORTANT TO YOUR BABY than any other piece of furniture in the nursery. A comfortable baby translates to a happy, sleeping baby, so vital in those first few months.

It's pretty simple to outfit a bed that meets your baby's needs. Select a firm mattress that fits snugly in the crib. Purchase fitted sheets that allow for shrinkage, as the elastic will need to fully cover the entire mattress. Purchase a bumper to protect baby's head until she can stand, and you're basically done.

But, oh, the fun you'll have when it comes to selecting bedding. An entire room can be fashioned around the crib, and modern options make it more fun than ever. Splurge, if you like. You deserve it. Because when it comes right down to it, adorable bedding is really just for mom and dad.

▲ ROMANTIC YET MODERN, this large, gregarious floral print is nursery appropriate in delicate shades of lilac and celery. A softly colored crib skirt adds to the romance.

◄ CRISP NAVY-AND-WHITE BEDDING with a surprise hit of lime makes for a tailored, classic ensemble. Tiny polka dots add a sweet, childlike accent.

UNIFYING THE DÉCOR

► WALL HANGINGS, PILLOWS, AND LAMPSHADES are an easy way to create an informal theme in a nursery. As your baby grows and interests change, they're easy to swap out without starting from scratch. Neutral furnishings allow for multiple rein-terpretations of the room.

▼ A GROWN-UP COLOR SCHEME feels restful, while circus motifs add a playful component. Patterned fabric pennants and pillows are easy do-it-yourself accents that complement the whimsical bedding. With decorating longevity in mind, only the crib will need to be replaced in a year or two.

Making the Most of Your Budget

UNLESS YOU PLAN TO REMODEL THE NURSERY **every few years**, you'll need to plan for the future right from the beginning. Your decorating dollars will best be spent on quality furniture that will adapt and last for years, such as a crib that converts into a youth bed or a changing table that can be used as a bookcase later.

Avoid age-specific design motifs in large parts of the room; choose timeless furnishings and wall treatments, then accessorize with baby items that can easily be swapped out. Forego wall-to-wall carpet in favor of area rugs that can be replaced when dirty or worn out.

When selecting accessories for the nursery, however, think beyond practical and opt for colors and patterns that you truly love. Gather photos for inspiration, along with color and fabric swatches. Sit with them for a while and you'll begin to see a pattern emerge, something you're drawn to over and over, whether a color or theme. Go with your instincts and you'll create a room you're happy to live with. And that's worth every penny you'll spend.

▲ BORROW A TRICK FROM DESIGNERS: Gather swatches and favorite objects for inspiration. Layer and rearrange until you find a combination that's visually compelling.

◄ THIS FORMER GUEST ROOM needed only the softening effect of pink to become suitable for a baby. Simple, graceful furniture and pale, solid fabrics offset the bold print of the wallpaper. Small touches of black unify the room without weighing it down.

► A BORDER ALONG THE TOP OF THE WALL visually produces the sense of a cozy, intimate space, as does the charming, casual furniture. The pink crib is balanced by the white bookcase, which prevents the room from being overwhelmed by rosy hues.

▼ WHIMSICAL AND TRADITIONAL PRINTS blend effortlessly in this nursery, the plaid picking up hues present in the printed fabric. Plaid, used sparingly, provides bold contrast. Fanciful printed fabric used on the grown-up chair creates a whimsical, child-friendly place for feedings, and later, bedtime stories.

Light Up Your Life

THE QUALITY OF LIGHT IN A NURSERY is important. Too much direct sunlight can interfere with naptime. A streetlight shining onto the crib at night poses the same problem. To alleviate such situations, make sure the crib is properly placed and windows fitted with blinds or shades.

Having minimal natural light in a nursery poses a different set of problems. It's excellent for sleep but can make the nursery feel heavy and, well, dark. In that case, you'll want to think of solutions to maximize what light there is. Use a pale sunny color, such as yellow, on the walls. Accent the room with table lamps, preferably with bulbs that simulate daylight. (However, you'll want to make sure that table lamps are out of reach when baby's old enough to pull them down.)

For every room, regardless of natural lighting, installing a dimmer switch on the overhead light is a worthwhile effort. It gives you the freedom to create the atmosphere you need at the time you need it.

▲ WHEN DEALING WITH AWKWARD AREAS such as skylights, the solution can easily become part of the décor. This skylight cover gives baby something to stimulate him visually, as well as allowing for total darkness when necessary.

◀ CHAIR-RAIL MOLDING creates an easy separation of paint and wallpaper, allowing the use of both and adding visual interest. The cheerful yellow energizes the pale, classic wallpaper, while the nursery colors are brought together in the old-fashioned rug, which gives the room a warm, cozy vibe.

▲ SMALL TOUCHES UNIFY A ROOM. Coordinating the fabric of a cushion with the fabric on a window shade creates a feeling of cohesion without being overly formal or stuffy. The knight theme feels classic rather than trendy, and the stenciled floor makes this traditional room more playful.

Flooring for Comfort and Safety

BABIES SPEND A LOT OF THEIR TIME ON THE FLOOR, especially once they've learned to crawl, so flooring has to meet high standards. It needs to be safe, comfortable for your baby, and easy for you to maintain.

Surprisingly, the safest surfaces are hard. Though it provides cushion, carpet also harbors allergens harmful to your baby. As for maintenance, hard floors are resilient and easier to keep clean. But where does that leave comfort?

A happy compromise is hard flooring, such as hardwood, accented with area rugs for both comfort and sound insulation. Rugs are easier to clean than carpet and easily replaceable if necessary. To add to their durability, consider using a fiber seal to repel spills and stains.

If you're looking for a clean, rather modern feel, sealed cork can work well in a nursery. It's sound absorbing, soft, and relatively easy to install. Of course, it too can be covered with a colorful area rug.

▶ A SOFT, NUBBY RUG is easy on baby's knees when crawling begins.

▲ MIXING PATTERNS isn't as tricky as it seems. You can freely mix florals with plaid and polka dots with stripes. Harmonizing the colors in each pattern allows for greater flexibility, even with busy prints. If your room is tiny, hang mirrors to visually enlarge the space as was done here.

▲ A TIMELESS ROOM, such as this one with its subtle wallpaper and classic furnishings, transitions easily from a nursery to a toddler's room. The canopy over the crib shades a sleeping baby from excessive light, while crib placement softens a sharp corner of the room, harmonizing it with its surroundings.

▲ FABRIC WALL COVERING establishes a soft, gentle, sound-insulated atmosphere. The painted ceiling and decorated wardrobe provide interesting images for the baby to survey when lying in the crib or being rocked in the chair.

▼ PLAN AHEAD WITH A SETUP LIKE THIS. When a diaper-changing area is needed, secure a changing station to the top of a 3-ft.- or 4-ft-high dresser. Once the station is outgrown, piggyback accessory drawers on the dresser top to gain extra storage.

▲ SIMPLE SHELVING FRAMES THIS CRIB and creates colorful display space. Dowels threaded through the shelving double as perches for stuffed animals and hanging rods for towels or receiving blankets.

◄ WITH ITS FENCE MOTIF, this radiator cover is more than a safety feature; it becomes a design asset, helping to create a lighthearted outdoorsy theme in the room. Several inches wider than the radiator, the cover also forms a convenient tabletop.

▶ FANCIFUL BUILT-INS AND PERKY COLORS create a joyful environment for a baby. But the room is prepared for a toddler, with generous play space, toy shelves, and a window seat. When the child reaches school age, the desk is ready and waiting.

▼ CALMING AND PLEASING FOR THE BABY, the soft colors, quiet patterns, and ceiling art in this room will remain appealing as the child grows. The changing table and bench will make easy transitions to a low dresser and a toy box respectively, both of which are accessible to a toddler or small child.

◀ INSTEAD OF A NURSERY that can be adapted for older kids, this is a grown-up room with the comforts of a nursery. The curtained niche is a cozy shelter for a crib or bed. The hanging couch—a Gloucester hammock—is a wonderful place to rock the baby now, but later it can be a guest bed or a place for kids to play or read.

▶ CIRCUMVENTING SAFETY HAZARDS, this room has shutters rather than drapery with pull cords and recessed lights rather than lamps with cords. The natural wool carpet is easy to vacuum, and the cotton rug is machine washable. Nontoxic ceramic tile covers the sill.

THEMED ROOMS

▶ A PAINTED MURAL elongates this small room and draws the eye into the valley beyond. The trees in the mural make the ceiling seem higher, while fanciful creatures keep baby company.

▲ THIS SOOTHING NURSERY is knit together from country and nature themes. Buttery yellow walls bring in the sunshine and offset the deep greens and browns present throughout the room. Touches of soft white add a crisp note.

▲ A PAINTED DRESSER BECOMES A CANVAS for artistic expression. Parents who lack painting skills can achieve the same effect by decoupaging cutouts to the front of the drawers. Tone-on-tone paint—the complementary greens—lightens the overall look.

▼ THIS LITTLE ALCOVE becomes a storage power-house when outfitted with a custom-built window seat that doubles as a changing table. Additional storage cabinets underneath provide plenty of space for toys. Later, it will be the perfect reading nook.

▲ A SMALL, AWKWARD CORNER feels cozy instead of claustrophobic with the addition of a painted ceiling, which neatly fills in for an overhead mobile. A coordinated storage bag on the crib makes maximum use of space, as does the decorative shelf on the wall.

▶ A VINTAGE LAMP is the foundation for this nursery-rhyme theme, carried out by cheerful printed fabric throughout the room. Simple, striped fabrics on the table and chair provide contrast but harmonize effortlessly. The basic yellow walls will allow for an easy redesign of the room in years to come.

▲ HEIRLOOMS AND HANDMADE GIFTS, such as this wall hanging/baby blanket, give a room personality. Display them instead of tucking them away in boxes. As baby outgrows such memorabilia, they can be archived for the next generation and replaced with more age-appropriate items.

▲ A CLASSIC STORYBOOK THEME gets carried over to decorative accents such as the lampshade, miniature figurines in the cabinet, and the vintage watering can. The glass at the back of the cabinet creates a sense of depth while showing off the wallpaper and complementing the delicate contents inside.

▲ INEXPENSIVE AND EASY do-it-yourself additions make the basics more exciting but still approachable and functional. Used in exacting ways, tiny patterned ribbons, like these gingham ones, stand out and create visual impact for a nursery window.

▲ BOLSTERED BY A STRONG DOSE OF WHITE, this whimsical wall-paper is still neutral enough to support strong patterns and colors in the room's fabrics. Surprising combinations, such as plaid and floral, mix readily and offer a traditional feel.

SIMPLE THEMED ELEMENTS

► THE CRIB itself becomes both the focus of the room and an instant heirloom with the addition of customized touches. The rug and curtains are easily obtained, solid basics that nevertheless support the Western feel, while charming printed bedding fully expresses this classic theme.

▼ STRONG, GRAPHIC BEDDING creates a playful mood in this otherwise subdued room. A simple pennant is easily constructed from fabric remnants and further defines the circus theme, while the coordinated chair fabric and bed skirt feel nicely matched without being too fussy.

▲ VINTAGE-STYLE THEMED BEDDING makes a strong impact and provides a solid foundation, while touches of blue and an antique mobile further reinforce this simple theme. The rustic wood furniture and floor echo the naturalistic, country-cabin feel and serve as a unifying element.

◄ ONE SIGNATURE PIECE can give an entire room focus. This vintage stork, found at a flea market, allows the nursery to take on a vintage feel without much effort. If combined with contemporary styling, it becomes a whimsical note.

ROOM TO GROW

Peel and Stick Art

IT CAN BE DIFFICULT TO COMMIT to a decorating scheme, particularly if you're a parent who craves change. Or perhaps commitment isn't your problem, but rather a self-perceived lack of artistic skill. In either case, peel and stick decals are an easy fix for a bare nursery or living space.

Decals come in borders, individual cutouts, and scenes, all with the ease of peel and stick application. Arrange a farm scene over a crib to create a focal point for the nursery, or use a decorative border over a changing table to distract your baby during diaper changes. Place designs around door frames or create patterned trim along the top of a wall.

Easily removed, decals won't strip paint or wallpaper and they can be rearranged countless times to satisfy your need for change or your inner perfectionist.

▶ PEEL AND STICK ART is perfect for a room meant to grow with your child. Swap out baby-oriented themes for more age-appropriate decals and you've got a versatile decorating solution.

Sharing a Bedroom with Baby

Not all new parents find themselves in a spacious home with an extra bedroom suitable for a nursery. Some are city dwellers living in small apartments and unable to move to a larger space. Others work from home, so that extra bedroom has already been transformed into an office or studio.

Of course, those parents will need to find new solutions as their child grows. But what about the first year of life; is it truly necessary to have a complete nursery? Are there ways to successfully integrate a baby into an existing household without wholesale renovation?

There are. Undoubtedly, they require compromise, but solutions don't have to lead to unhappiness. Basically, pare your needs down to the essentials and get as organized as possible. In the end, you'll have less clutter to deal with and peaceful cohabitation—at least for a little while.

▼ ▶ PARENTS AND BABY CAN EASILY SHARE SPACE in the first months of life. The keys to peaceful cohabitation are simple, practical furnishings and a soothing palette. Organized storage keeps everything at hand while visually keeping chaos at bay.

▲ A SOPHISTICATED PALETTE of
chocolate brown and warm, pale
blue appeals to all ages. Classic
childhood elements, such as this
cuddly teddy bear, soften the crisp,
modern graphics of the bed pillows,
synthesizing the adult and child features of the room.

▲ A SIMPLE, SPARE ROCKER fits easily in tight spaces. A cushion and a
blanket make nighttime feedings more comfortable, while an ottoman does
double-duty as a table with the simple addition of a moveable tray.

Creating Storage

BABIES COME INTO THIS WORLD WITH NOTHING and quickly accumulate more material possessions than their parents. There are seemingly endless numbers of onesies, socks, hats, diapers, and toys to contend with. And let's not forget all the gear that starts to creep in and take over your household!

The solution is, quite simply, proper storage. But think beyond walk-in closets; aside from the fact that your nursery may not have one, walk-ins keep everything hidden behind numerous doors. Exposed storage can be attractive as well as more accessible. Armoires can replace closets, and furniture such as changing tables can do double-duty as extra storage.

The bottom line is that you'll need even more storage space than you think you do. Children's possessions grow exponentially, and what seemed adequate in the beginning won't feel like much later on. Don't hesitate to create as much storage in a room as you possibly can. You'll need it.

▲ EXPOSED STORAGE CAN BE ATTRACTIVE with a diffusing element, such as the wire mesh front of this cabinet. Textured baskets and painted boxes further serve to tidy up storage and keep the overall look comfortable instead of cluttered.

▲ THIS SPARE BUT FULLY FUNCTIONAL changing table handles overflow from a small bedroom closet. Deep shelves store multiple outfits, while shelves and hooks placed above the changing table create a space for accessories and small keepsakes.

◄ STORAGE OPTIONS ARE ENDLESS in this nursery, with its large dresser, painted storage bench, and customized closet. The converted bookcase placed in the closet keeps items well organized while adding additional storage space on top.

▼ SMALL SPACES require efficiently used vertical storage. This narrow stand triples the storage space with removable pails that can hold everything from small toys to grooming supplies, hats, and shoes.

◄ IF HIDDEN STORAGE IS MORE YOUR STYLE, this convertible changing table offers curtains for hidden storage, which also soften the look of utilitarian furniture. Storage cubbies on the removable top keep small items handy. Later, the table can be used as a bookcase.

▲ A LAUNDRY BASKET outfitted with a decorative liner becomes an attractive abode for stuffed animals. Other toys requiring adult supervision are stored in a whimsically painted dumbwaiter with a safety latch.

◄ OPEN BINS MAKE BABY'S TOYS ACCESSIBLE while keeping them separate and less cluttered. Lining the bins with squares of oilcloth is not only a decorative touch; it makes cleanup from sticky fingers a cinch.

▲ A LARGE STORAGE UNIT keeps everything readily accessible. Dresser drawers provide ample room for clothing, and the lit space between drawers and shelves serves as a tidy changing area. Small cubbyholes store toys separately and in easy reach of baby.

▲ MOST PARENTS END UP with clothing their infants haven't yet grown into. Keep closets clutter-free by storing extra clothing in straight-sided wicker baskets, hidden under a bench or other piece of standing furniture. Baskets can be used later for extra toy storage.

▲ SIMPLE TEXTURES AND A COAT OF PAINT add to the charm of these exposed storage containers without detracting from their usefulness. Blankets can be rolled and stored in baskets, either solid or open, like this one, while clothing and bedding are better in bins that allow air to circulate.

▶ SMALL NURSERIES require creative storage solutions. In this room, storage is amplified with the use of wire baskets stored under the crib. The bed skirt just obscures the tops of the baskets, letting their texture shine but keeping the view clean, not cluttered.

▲ THE ADDITION OF RODS ON A CHANGING TABLE
creates hanging space for extra blankets and other large
items. Decorative flowerpots are an inexpensive solution
for holding small items, such as ointments and creams,
while an attractive basket keeps extra clothing nearby for
those inevitable accidents.

◄ A SMALL BEDROOM CLOSET becomes
a storage workhorse when fitted with customized shelves. Vertical storage promotes
maximum usage, while shelves under
hanging clothes keep clutter off the floor
and provide space for a laundry basket.
A small bottom drawer filled with toys
delights a curious baby.

Making the Most of an Armoire

AN ARMOIRE IS ONE OF THE MOST VERSATILE pieces of furniture, particularly for a baby's room. Most come with a clothes rod and shelves, allowing hung and folded clothing items to be stored in the same place. Plus, the shelves closest to the floor can be outfitted with bins and baskets for baby to get into. Stuff these with soft toys or even socks and shoes, giving your baby her first experience at learning where to find and store things she'll want to use every day. Best of all, armoires come complete with doors, so that you can close up any mess quickly!

▲ WOODEN SOCK DRAWERS, painted to match the room's décor, are the perfect size for pint-size clothing. Use them to store rows of onesies or tiny shoes and socks, notorious for getting separated from their partners.

▲ WALLPAPER APPLIED TO THE BACK of this armoire brings unexpected charm to a functional piece. Shelves placed a bit lower than usual provide ample room for shoes and accessories to be stored underneath the hanging clothes.

▲ A HANGING ORGANIZER customized with colorful fabric remnants serves as a useful catchall. It doesn't take up much space, but is perfect for bibs, small toys and books, and other accessories you want to keep close at hand.

▲ FULLY OUTFITTED, this delightful armoire replaces a built-in closet. The small space is functional and efficient, with organized contents contained in boxes and bins. Storage on the doors maximizes every inch of space, while special toys and keepsakes can be displayed on top.

2

Bedrooms for Toddlers

Toddlers are exuberant, exciting creatures. They're busy learning, exploring, and asserting their independence. They adore repetition, yet have short attention spans. They're imaginative, creative, messy, and full of energy. They can be, by turns, delightful then monstrous.

The best toddler rooms manage to cater to their ever-changing needs while providing a sense of stability and structure. Striking colors and patterns appeal to them visually, accessible toys and storage allow them control over their environment, and a cozy bed with a favorite friend or two helps the restless toddler settle down. Toddlers also appreciate plenty of floor space for free play, a reading area, a place for arts and crafts, and an area for dress-up and make-believe.

Fantasy is right at home in the toddler's room, too, because kids of this age group so easily move between what is real and what is imaginary. Murals, fanciful furniture, nooks, and hideaways all set the stage for grand adventures.

On a practical level, the best toddler rooms will grow and change as your child does. During these busy years, frequent redecorating will probably be less and less appealing. Crafting an easily transformable environment makes sense. Before you know it, your little toddler will be heading off for his first day of school!

◄ CREATIVITY IS ENCOURAGED with accessible zones for building, arts and crafts, and reading. Paint and simple patterns create a cheerful, coordinated suite of furniture. The bed is tucked into a corner, making it cozy and unobtrusive and allowing room for free play.

▲ BIG, BOLD SHAPES ARE EASY for small children to understand. Exaggerated sizes and forms give this transitional nursery–toddler room a fanciful, Alice-in-Wonderland quality. The low table is practical as well as fun, and the overscale knobs, easy for toddlers to handle, can be replaced later as the kids grow up.

◄ A DYNAMICALLY SHAPED ROOM can be as much fun as the toys it contains. Every curve, triangle, and corner of this room invites interaction, functioning as either a storage place or a play zone. The airplane bed with wing shelf turns the deep angle of the wall to advantage.

▲ A HOUSE IS ONE OF THE FIRST SHAPES kids recognize and is a perennial favorite with the younger set. The triangular roof shape of this wall transforms the whole room into a fun, kid-friendly space. The wall also tempers the bed's exposure to light and forms a display area. The space-saving cabinet echoes the triangle theme.

▶ INSPIRED NOTCHES—from the little bedside-wall cutouts to the window bay—give this room personality. A recess between built-in closets makes an inviting play niche. Hooks in the niche hold playthings now, but later the space can be used as a dressing area.

Quick and Easy Highlights

Looking for design ideas that are easy on the wallet and simple to implement? Try these.

- Garnish the walls with game boards or game pieces from your toddler's favorite games or with simple constructions made from colorful, flat building blocks.

- Ring the room with bright pegs or hooks at chair-rail height. They are both decorative and functional; use them to hang hats, souvenirs, blue ribbons, stuffed animals, framed pictures, or small shelves.

- Cut down the legs of an old table and coat it with glossy paint to craft a game table or hobby center.

- Line painted orange crates with quilted fabric. They make handy bins for toys, books, even socks.

- Spray-paint baskets of different shapes and sizes to hold everything from large toys to building sets to crayons. Baskets with handles can hang on wall hooks.

▼ TODDLERS LIKE OBJECTS THEY CAN TOUCH, so the bright cutout plywood octopus, submarine, and waves on this bed are perfect for a child who loves playing in the water. Automotive paint gives the cutouts a hard, durable surface. Toddlers also like personalized things, hence the undersea mural featuring his pet dog and cats.

▲ BIG, COLORFUL PLANES AND CARS make this space-efficient suite of built-ins feel friendly for a toddler. Made of ³⁄₈-in. medium-density fiberboard (MDF), they can be removed when the child is older, leaving handsome cherry cabinetry with colorful veneer edging and wood knobs.

▶ THIS ROOM IS OUTFITTED WITH FUN, flexible furnishings including a fold-down play surface on the right that rests on an open drawer. The bus-themed bench/radiator cover encloses toy boxes. A foam mattress nests inside another with a foam ring; without the inner mattress, it works as a transitional bed for a toddler.

Choosing Colors

▲ WHAT CAN YOU DO if your child's bedroom is small but her doll collection is big? Build a dollhouse headboard with inset shelves. This plywood structure has three shelf levels and a dynamic array of windows.

WHAT COLORS ARE BEST for a child's room? The answer depends partly on the room and partly on the child's nature. Light colors expand space and darks lend intimacy. Cool colors such as blues and greens are soothing, while warm reds, oranges, and yellows are stimulating.

By age three or four, children have favorite colors. Be daring; use these colors to give their rooms a personal flavor. To find a winning palette, display crayons in the six primary and secondary colors (red, yellow, blue, orange, green, purple) and ask the child to choose her favorite. Next, ask for a second and third choice. Sort through more crayons or paint chips in related shades to refine the choices.

The least intense shade probably is best as the dominant room color. Use another favorite color for a third of the room's finishes, such as on molding or cabinetry. Top off the scheme with accents in the third tone. Before settling on colors, look at large paint swatches in the room throughout the day and evening and under different lighting to ensure the colors you choose stay true and appealing.

▲ A SIMPLE DEVICE—painting one wall yellow and the other blue—gives this room personality and verve. Drawers in a yellow and blue checkerboard play off the theme, as do the slide-out plastic toy storage bins in box frames.

▶ INSPIRATION FOR the colors and the graphics used in this room came from playful window-covering fabric. Cars, trains, and other painted images soar high on the wall and even on the ceiling, leaving wall space open for pictures. An oil or latex glaze gives the walls and ceiling a light, watercolor effect.

▲ THOUGH RELATIVELY INEXPENSIVE, the three-dimensional elements in this room add a magical touch. Leaves and apples cut from cloth hang on the painted tree and on actual tree branches arranged around the room. Lightly padded fabric shingles give dimensional heft to the awning. The curtain holdbacks are flowers made of cloth-covered wire.

▲ SHELVES BECOME THE HIGHLIGHT of the room when they look like something kids love. This mock tree house is a display surface for toys.

Themed Rooms

Y THE AGE OF THREE OR FOUR, children have distinct preferences and are generally able to communicate those desires, which means that they can participate in selecting themes for their rooms. Often, however, a toddler will want a room that focuses on an action figure or cartoon character he's grown to love. A couple of months and a full suite of themed accessories later, he's moved on to the next thing. Transcending the mass-market product blitz makes sense if you're looking to create an environment with staying power. That doesn't mean you shouldn't give in to a three-year-old's desires, but a printed pillow, themed lampshade, or large toy are often enough to satisfy his demands.

For longevity, the best themes are classic and easily adaptable. A room theme can be motivated by a color, the region the family calls home, a favorite pastime, a special heirloom, or a unique find—whatever creates a story and provides a haven.

▲ WHAT WAS ONCE A CHARMING NURSERY with a themed mural easily transforms into a toddler's room courtesy of a convertible crib. Simple wood furniture, taken from other parts of the house, blend easily in these storybook woods. The butterflies overhead add a colorful, tactile element.

▶ LIVELY PAINTED FURNITURE is an easy do-it-yourself project, even for those not artistically inclined. Simple patterns like stripes and checkerboards are created by blocking off areas with painter's tape. The pale yellow walls are a surprising and delightful background for this crisp, classic color scheme.

Painted Effects

Paint can work wonders in a room. Use it to design themes, create special effects and textures, enlarge a space or make it more intimate, or emphasize or deemphasize light. It's probably the most versatile and exciting tool you can invest in.

Think outside the box; paint the ceiling a different (but paler) color than the walls, quickly and inexpensively bring a shabby hardwood floor back to life, or create two-toned furniture.

If you feel intimidated by the idea of do-it-yourself painting projects, purchase paint and tools from a reputable home center and gather as much information from knowledgeable employees as you can. Before you know it, you'll be a pro.

▲ BOLD DOTS POP AGAINST WHITE WALLS. Stencils were made from squares of easily removable, self-adhesive vinyl with circles cut out of the middle. Color was stippled onto the wall to minimize leakage under the stencil, and the stencil was removed after the paint had dried.

▲ A PAINTED WALL GETS A BIT OF TEXTURE with a dragging technique above the chair rail molding, achieved with a long, coarse-bristled brush. Bottom panels are accented with casually painted stripes.

◄ A PATTERNED BORDER painted directly onto the hardwood floor adds visual interest and structure to the open floor space. The design is sealed with floor sealer, protecting the paint and making cleanup a snap.

▶ A SPONGE-PAINTED BLUE GLAZE creates an ethereal ceiling with a soothing effect. Vintage accessories and simple furnishings keep the overall look light and clean and can be adapted easily as this child gets older. Plenty of open floor space gives him ample room to play.

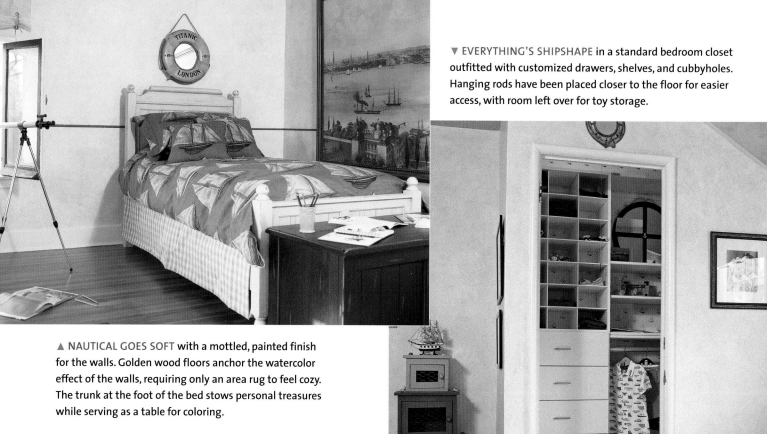

▼ EVERYTHING'S SHIPSHAPE in a standard bedroom closet outfitted with customized drawers, shelves, and cubbyholes. Hanging rods have been placed closer to the floor for easier access, with room left over for toy storage.

▲ NAUTICAL GOES SOFT with a mottled, painted finish for the walls. Golden wood floors anchor the watercolor effect of the walls, requiring only an area rug to feel cozy. The trunk at the foot of the bed stows personal treasures while serving as a table for coloring.

▲ THIS FANTASY ROOM leaves no stone unturned, with decorative painting on ceiling and walls and vibrant patterns everywhere. The look stays lively instead of overwhelming due to the liberal doses of white. Curtains hung from the bed frame create the illusion of an extra window.

◄ PAINTED DRAWERS echo the vibrant colors found in the room's palette, colors that are stimulating and visually interesting to young children. Bug-themed knobs are an appropriate, whimsical touch for this garden bedroom.

▼ A FUNKY CHANDELIER was the source of inspiration for this vibrant and extravagant room, providing color and design clues. Unique finds provide a strong focal point for a themed room and create a personal, rather than mass-market, feel.

▼ A PAINTED BORDER above a picture rail makes a potent impact in this room without weighing it down. A similar effect can be achieved with a wallpaper border and is easily replaced as your child grows. Details like the zebra-print lamp add to the fun.

▶ NO DETAIL IS OVER-LOOKED in this exuberant jungle room. A grown-up bed is balanced by the whimsical table and chairs meant only for child's play. A long window seat encourages animal exploration, while deep drawers hold the accoutrements of adventure.

▲ A DEEP-RED WALL provides a dramatic backdrop for this nautical theme. Open windows suffuse the room with natural light and prevent the red from feeling heavy. White furnishings, ceilings, and trim keep the overall effect crisp and graphic, while cheerful fabrics add a playful note.

▶ A SOOTHING MURAL DRAWS THE EYE beyond the boundary of the wall, making this room appear larger. Sandy, neutral carpeting and walls complement the sea theme, while shades of blue are echoed in the furniture and accents. A simple bookcase also makes a handy nightstand.

▲ ADULT FURNISHINGS GET A MAKEOVER fit for a knight. A basic bookcase gets a *trompe l'oeil* treatment, and a decorative wooden cutout mounted to the wall creates a compact headboard. A game table awaits future chess matches, while the open floor space and low-weave carpet provide a solid surface for toddler play.

Themes on a Budget

THEMES CAN EASILY BE CREATED THROUGH ACCESSORIZING ALONE. The bed frame, nightstand, overhead shelf, and neutral rug are common to all of the rooms shown here, but simple, minimal details completely change the tone of each room, demonstrating how easy it will be to reinvent in the future.

The key is to invest in bold elements that make a powerful impact in a basic room. Patterned bedding creates a strong focal point. A few well-chosen themed items placed close to the bed easily reinforce the idea, as groupings of like items tend to make more of an impact than small pieces on their own.

Another idea is to create a themed corner, especially if your child has her heart set on something that will quickly become dated. Create a charming reading nook with a themed lampshade and chair cushion along with relevant books. It's a budget-conscious solution you'll both be able to live with.

▲ THE SMALL AREA RUG punches up neutral flooring and makes a strong statement. The bedspread and blanket echo the colors found in the rug, while a printed sheet and pillowcase create a distinct theme. Framed robot prints tie the look together, as does the robot collection on display.

▲ THEMED BEDDING CREATES A STRONG FOCAL POINT for this rodeo bedroom, while the lampshade, clock, and bedside frame are tied in with additional vintage-style western fabrics.

▲ VIBRANT FLORAL BEDDING accessorized by a backdrop of mod dots and a flower-themed lamp create a girlish room that's stylish, not overly sweet.

Multiuse Bedrooms

MANY HOMES DON'T HAVE SPACE FOR A DEDICATED PLAY-ROOM, making a toddler's bedroom the center of her universe. It's here that she sleeps, plays, perhaps watches television, reads, builds, engages in arts and crafts, and entertains playmates.

Organized storage plays a starring role in the multiuse bedroom, especially toy storage, which should be easily accessible for a child. Toddlers tend to feel frustrated when they're unable to reach something by themselves, and it's easier for a parent to teach a toddler how to help clean his room when there are specific areas for toys and other belongings.

Another consideration is how to set up activity zones within a room; furniture that does double duty can help. A headboard bookcase easily combines the sleeping and reading area. A small table can double as a building zone and a place for coloring or drawing. If possible, it's also nice if at least part of the flooring is composed of something easily cleaned. That way, children can finger paint or play with modeling clay without incident.

▲ A WINDING BEACH PATH in the mural is echoed in the flooring, creating the illusion that it continues into the room, complementing this long, narrow space. The built-in platform is equipped with multiple drawers for toy storage, while the bed frame is replaced with multilevel shelving and built-ins.

▶ A CHEERFUL TEEPEE BECOMES A CLEVER HIDEAWAY within this bedroom. Uncovered windows bring in light and integrate nature with the simple, earthy furnishings. The bold use of color on the teepee and wall accents infuses energy into the neutrals that dominate most of the room.

◄ A SMALL BEDROOM BECOMES SPACIOUS with the construction of a loft, placed in front of a window for extra light. Steps lead to the bed, protected by decorative railings. Vertical storage uses space efficiently, leaving room for a special hideaway under the loft and a cozy reading corner.

▼ BUILT-INS MAKE USE OF AWKWARD SPACE in this small bedroom, with shelving that follows the sloping line of the ceiling, maximizing vertical space. A window seat provides extra play space as well as storage, while a bookshelf nestled against the footboard keeps toys close at hand.

▲ STORAGE OPTIONS ABOUND in this multiuse room. Storage steps built in behind the bed serve as both a headboard and a play area. Sliding covers make books and toys easy to access and easy to tuck away. A reading light encourages bedtime stories.

▲ PAINTED CABINETS, BOLTED TO THE WALL, easily become part of the décor with a bit of paint and also keep clutter at bay. Overturned paint cans make clever chairs for a kid-size table, and the faux-stone floor disguises smudges and dirt, making it perfect for a rough-and-tumble kid.

▲ OFFERING AMPLE SPACE FOR SELF-EXPRESSION, fabric-covered cork squares allow for an ever-changing personal tableau. Cherished memorabilia can be kept safe near the top, while bottom squares give a toddler his own exhibit space.

ROOM TO GROW

From Babyproofing to Childproofing

YOUR TODDLER STILL NEEDS THE SAFETY PRECAUTIONS that were put into place when he was an infant. However, there's a new problem to contend with. Toddlers are constantly moving; they love to run and jump, and they especially love to climb. To ward off accidents, secure high dressers and bookcases to the wall.

Toddlers are also notorious for jumping on the bed. Make sure the bed isn't placed too close to a window and that all windows have safety guards and security latches.

▲ WHEN CHILDREN SHARE A SMALL ROOM, efficient storage helps keep the peace. Tall, twin bookshelves provide individual areas for displaying books and special items, while ample drawer space keeps clothing separate. Additional drawers (one for each child) under the window seat hold toys.

▲ RETRO STYLING AND A CLASSIC BASEBALL MOTIF create a comfortable room that's coordinated but not stuffy, suitable for brothers with an age gap. The storage headboard on the top bunk keeps prized possessions away from a curious toddler, while small toys are easily stored under the bottom bunk.

▲ A FANCIFUL DRESSING AREA is designed with longevity in mind. Separate cabinets keep the peace between sisters, while the communal dressing table allows plenty of space for dress-up and makeovers. Additional cubbies overhead display faithful friends.

▶ DECORATED IN A BOLD PALETTE, this room is ageless. Iron bed frames take up less space than a bulky wood type would and keep the emphasis on color. The demitable bolted to the wall creates a sense of separation, while the overhead cornices lend a royal touch. Full bed skirts hide underbed storage.

▲ THIS CONVERTED ATTIC SPACE easily lends itself to sharing. Simple and clean, each side mirrors the other. The pair of windows provides equal light, while the cozy bench serves as communal space. Cleverly placed tables work as nightstands or set the stage for a tea party.

◄ SIMPLE, STREAMLINED FURNITURE and a large, well-placed window and skylight keep this tiny converted attic room from feeling claustrophobic. The small window seat makes a cozy niche to curl up in, with a view of the sky overhead. A low-pile rug allows comfortable floor play.

▲ A STURDY BUT DECORATIVE SIDE RAIL protects a wiggly sleeper, while the patterned bedspreads add a needed burst of color. Heavy, painted furniture suits rowdy boys; it's balanced by pale, subtly patterned walls that reflect light, adding a sunny glow.

▲ A PAINTED FLOOR BORDER with a Parcheesi® game at the corner adds visual interest and complements the pattern of the bedroom rug. Different game boards are painted in the other corners of the room.

▲ SATISFYING A CHILD'S WHIM, a favorite book and television character graces a high, heavy dresser that's bolted to the wall for safety. While fitting for now, it can easily be repainted when the infatuation wanes.

▲ A PALETTE OF COOL BLUE AND PALE YELLOW accented by happy bursts of red appeals to a toddler's love of color. Curtains over each headboard create an atmosphere of privacy, while individual benches give each child some personal space. Communal items, such as the train table, encourage shared play.

◄ EASY, PAINTED CANVASES can make a big impact and provide a punch of color where needed. Create your own art by painting simple patterns onto canvas or by using stencils and a ruler if your freehand style isn't to your liking.

▲ CHILDREN HAVE FREE REIN in what had been unused attic space. The unique architectural lines of the room mesh easily with the casual décor. Beds are tucked away under the ceiling vault, with a separate area for reading, movies, and play.

► A CUSTOM-BUILT PLATFORM affords privacy as well as storage in this small space. A divided closet takes up half the platform, while the other half houses a bed with a headboard shelf for personal possessions. A divided bulletin board gives each child a place to exhibit special items.

A Note about Bunk Beds

BUNK BEDS ARE INVALUABLE IN A SHARED ROOM; they make efficient use of floor space and allow kids a sense of separation. Top bunks aren't for toddlers! However, your toddler can sleep on the bottom bunk if you have children of different ages sharing a room—if you have twins, wait on the bunk beds until they're at least six.

As always, safety is an issue. Buy a bed with protective railings on the top bunk for young children, and make sure the mattress is securely fastened to the bed.

▶ MANY BUNK BEDS are available with a protective railing incorporated into the design. Check to make sure it's sturdy and covers most, if not all, of the length of the bed.

▼ TONE-ON-TONE BLUE with accents of red and white create an uplifting color scheme. The starry sky overhead complements the recessed lighting, and even the ceiling fan seems like a natural part of the décor. Area rugs add a touch of color and design to the neutral carpeting.

▲ A BUILT-IN BED MAKES USE OF AWKWARD SPACE, creating a cozy niche that feels private, even in a shared room. Drawers under the bed offer a safe hiding place for storybooks and treasured possessions. The pint-size closet keeps toys out of sight.

▲ KIDS LOVE PERSONALIZED ITEMS, and with customized chairs there's no argument over what belongs to whom. A small trunk works as a side table, keeping a lamp at child level, while the comfy kid-size chairs promote reading and conversation. A handmade, fabric-covered memo board provides space for keepsakes.

▲ A GENEROUSLY SCALED ROOM provides multiple comforts for bunkmates. The rough-hewn beds include clever accents like the built-in night table and underbed drawers. A daybed works as a place to relax and watch television or host sleepovers in the future.

▲ COMFORT AND COLOR ARE KEY in this warm and vibrant bedroom. The textured wall color resembles washed denim, while punches of red liven things up. A hand-me-down rug feels right at home in the reading area, warming up the neutral carpet. Rope accents add a playful note.

Sharing a Room with Baby

SOMETIMES SHARING A ROOM WITH A SIBLING is the only option when a new baby comes along. The greatest dilemma is often space. To make the most efficient use of space, try limiting nursery furniture to a crib, a changing pad on top of a dresser, and an area for storage. If there isn't a nursing chair already in the room, consider having one in another room where you won't wake up your toddler during late-night feedings.

Of course, safety precautions must be in place for both ages, and when your new baby is old enough to crawl you will probably need to move your toddler's small toys into a family room or make sure the baby is never left alone in the bedroom. Safety gates can help in this arena.

As far as décor goes, consider timeless options without baby motifs. Pastels work fine in a shared room, especially when punched up with brighter accents scattered around for more impact. Also think about giving greater weight to the toddler's desires, as your newborn won't care what color or style dominates the room.

▼ BATHED IN PINK, this room is girly but not babyish, with bright pink accents amping up the overall décor. Simple white frames for both the twin bed and the crib keep the room from looking overly crowded while unifying the furnishings. A tea table gives a toddler some space of her own.

◄ A TRADITIONALLY BOYISH COLOR SCHEME mixed with a floral border and oversized gingham curtains and bed skirt nicely bridges the gender gap in a room shared by a baby boy and his older sister. The dark bed frame visually separates the bedroom area from the nursery area.

Furnishings

NEVER BEFORE HAS THERE BEEN so much furniture designed especially for children: small tables and chairs, diminutive bookcases, and fantasy furniture resembling everything from castles to tree houses. Children love this kind of furniture; it gives them permission to play and makes them feel right at home in their house.

However, scaled-down kids' furniture should be balanced with larger pieces in a room. Chairs and tables can easily be swapped out for larger pieces when your child has grown; an entire suite of small furniture, however, makes for a very expensive renovation.

When selecting fantasy furniture, opt for a classic theme your child can live with for a few years. Such pieces are rarely inexpensive, so you'll want to choose wisely. Another option is to decorate basic furniture with a painted motif that reflects your child's current passion. When your child outgrows the design, a fresh coat of paint provides instant transformation.

▲ OVERSIZE KNOBS ARE PERFECT for a toddler's clumsy grasp, while their whimsical design and color liven up a plain dresser. Later, they can be easily replaced by more age-appropriate hardware.

► A PINT-SIZE STORAGE BENCH makes a private reading area suitable only for a child. Fanciful wall painting makes seating appear even more diminutive; the oversize orchid on a tiny chair contributes to the Alice in Wonderland effect.

► THIS ROOM FEATURES A REPLICA of mom and dad's reading area, but it's just the right fit for their young son. The bookcase is scaled down to work with the small club chair. A table lamp above is set out of reach of a toddler's curious hands while still shining light onto storybooks.

▼ A WHIMSICAL, CLEVERLY DESIGNED TRAIN BED isn't just for show; it's a storage power-house, with a toy box built into the front, head-board shelves that hold petite passengers, and a side cabinet for stowing small treasures. Now, the trundle bed protects a toddler who may fall out of bed, but it will be useful for overnight guests later.

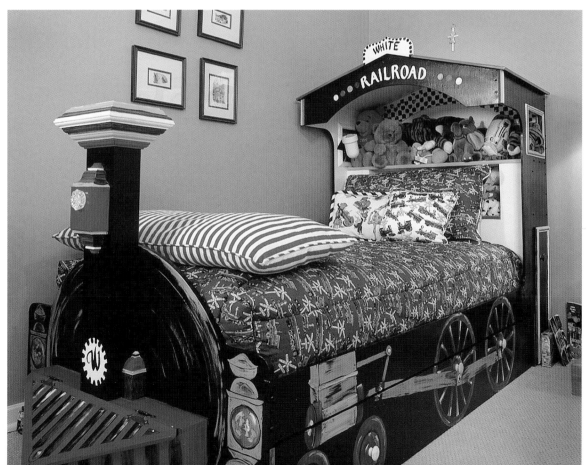

▼ A STRAY CHAIR TAKES ON NEW LIFE in a toddler's room. The bars make it easy for a little one to get a foothold, while the padded cushion provides comfort and protection from hard edges and also adds a youthful touch.

▲ THIS VERSATILE STORAGE HEADBOARD offers something to occupy your little one when sleep isn't an option. A safety rail keeps overhead books from tumbling down, and small cubbies provide a safe haven for a few sleeping buddies.

▲ A COZY BUILT-IN forms an enveloping nook for a small child. A mounted reading light encourages bedtime stories, while underbed drawers contribute to storage.

▲ SEPARATE PIECES OF FURNITURE look substantial when grouped together. Individual storage units bookend the desk, perfect for a room shared by two. The desk can accommodate two chairs, if needed, for side-by-side play. Later, it'll make a good study area.

Fun with Paint and Decoupage

Painted furniture is perfect for kids' rooms; it's an easy way to add texture, pattern, color, and a touch of whimsy. It's also a good way to rescue thrift store finds or household furniture well past its prime.

Though it may look intimidating, even a novice can paint furniture. Take the minimalist approach and paint an old dresser a solid color, then add colorful hardware. Utilize painter's tape to create stripes, checks, or plaid. Use stencils for perfect polka dots or a more difficult pattern.

Decoupage also works well with painted furniture: Decoupage wallpaper remnants to the fronts of dresser drawers; apply patterned paper silhouettes to chairs or a simple bed frame.

For durability, sand furniture, if necessary, then prime with a latex primer followed by the paint of your choice. For best results, use semigloss enamel paint. If you're decoupaging, apply the desired cutouts to painted furniture with decoupage medium, then seal the entire area with more.

▶ ALL THE PIECES SHOWN HERE started out as unfinished furniture or lackluster finds at a yard sale. Spruced up with paint, decoupage, and decorative hardware, they rival more expensive customized furniture found in select boutiques.

ORGANIZING THE SPACE

◄ A LOW CEILING creates a cozy niche that will be a magnet for small children. To define the niche as a play space, everything—mirror, lamp, and bookshelves—is at toddler height.

▼ THE BOOKCASE PARTITION neatly organizes this room into sleeping and activity areas, leaving plenty of floor space for playing. Toy bins are accessible but behind cabinet doors to reduce clutter. The top bunk can be used for play space too, and the lamp-post makes fun lighting.

Montessori at Home

THE MONTESSORI SYSTEM—which is aimed at helping young children develop mentally, physically, and socially through learning in a nonrestrictive, kid-friendly environment—has a place at home as well as in the classroom. Montessori experts say young children learn by observing and voluntarily practicing skills. They also say that children up to age six function best in familiar, organized surroundings where they can freely choose activities.

In a child's room, this means that tables and chairs should be kid-size and shelves for toys and books should be low, making it easy for kids to do what they want and find what they need. Toy bins should be labeled by picture, word, and/or color so that children can keep their playthings organized. Same goes for clothing storage.

These strategies will help your child pick up skills, learn good habits, develop responsibility, and feel proud of her accomplishments.

▲ TO CAPTURE EVERY INCH of activity space, most of the storage in this bedroom—including "dresser drawers"—was moved into the closet. The only thing the kids will outgrow in this closet arrangement is the low hanging rod; it can be replaced or topped with a second rod as needed.

▲ AN IMAGINATIVE STRUCTURE like this adds both storage and play space. Kids can climb on the truck or play games on its tabletops. The storage sections include a toy box, large slide-out drawers with rims to keep toys from falling out, and a shallow desk compartment.

◄ WHEN SPICED UP with a cheery pattern or washed in a toddler's favorite colors, simple shelves or pegboards become fun to use.

► BENCH SHELVES keep books and toys visible yet put away. Another advantage is that they store things close to the floor where toddlers sit and play. The seat pad is easily replaced as kids grow and their tastes change.

▲ SPRINKLED ACROSS THE WALL, small storage cubes work as decorative accents and resting places for kids' stuff. To personalize them, line the boxes with bright paint, paper, or children's art.

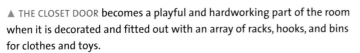

▲ THE CLOSET DOOR becomes a playful and hardworking part of the room when it is decorated and fitted out with an array of racks, hooks, and bins for clothes and toys.

3

Bedrooms for Kids

I t may be called a bedroom, but a child's room is, of course, much more than that. It's where the child sleeps and plays, where she dresses and studies, and where she can go to be with friends or spend some solo time. The best kids' bedrooms are shaped around all of these functions and around the kids themselves—their ages, interests, personalities, and imaginations.

The younger the child, the more simple the room should be. A toddler is happy with a few open toy bins at floor level, while most preteens need ample shelving and drawer space. A small child's room should have zones readied for crafts, games, and reading, as well as generous floor space for active play. Older children don't need such compartmentalized areas, but their rooms should still have at least three zones: for homework, for sitting with friends, and for sleeping.

Every child welcomes a place to relax or decompress. Reserve the quietest, coziest corner for that retreat, then structure the rest of the room around it. Platforms, two-sided cabinetry, and archways help define different zones, while lofts, nooks, pass-throughs, and secret hide-aways add intrigue.

There's no need to puzzle over a theme for the room. Ask your children; they'll know exactly what they want.

◀ WHIMSICAL HIGHLIGHTS, such as the picketed bed boards and the birdhouse bedposts and wall-mounted shelves, turn a practical bedroom into a secret garden. A palette of outdoorsy colors knits the room together. The jumbo window seat with under-bench drawers is one play center; the toy box and chair form another.

Grade School Districts

LIFE IS BIG AND BOLD for grade school children. They are making new friends, discovering new interests and activities, embracing the latest fads, and delighting in make-believe. That's why bold ideas are just right for a schoolchild's bedroom.

Bring on the jungle animals or dinosaurs, castles or butterflies, mermaids or cowboys. Go ahead with the vibrant colors and trompe l'oeil scenes. Go all out with canopy beds fit for princesses and mosquito-netted safari cots fit for little adventurers. Kids this age love surroundings drenched with atmosphere.

They also invest energy and enthusiasm in the sports and hobbies they've developed an interest in. Set up part of the room as a dedicated space for sports equipment, model plane projects, or jewelry making. Incorporate shelves and display walls around the room for handiwork, collections, posters, and prizes.

▲ HAVING A ROOM under the eaves is fun; having one with a dormer window and a cozy bed niche is even more so. White walls brighten the room while tinted ceilings lend intimacy, especially in the niche. Under-seat toy drawers and built-in bookshelves provide storage without absorbing floor space.

▲ SHEETS OF PERFORATED HARDBOARD can easily be cut to size to make a wall for displaying and stowing a child's belongings. Strong enough to support laden shelves, bins, and baskets, the panels also can hold pictures, movable hooks, and a changing exhibit of collectibles.

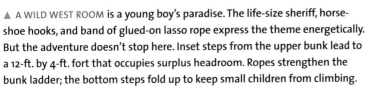

▲ A WILD WEST ROOM is a young boy's paradise. The life-size sheriff, horse-shoe hooks, and band of glued-on lasso rope express the theme energetically. But the adventure doesn't stop here. Inset steps from the upper bunk lead to a 12-ft. by 4-ft. fort that occupies surplus headroom. Ropes strengthen the bunk ladder; the bottom steps fold up to keep small children from climbing.

THEMES AND VARIATIONS

▲ THIS ROOM WILL BE SIMPLE to change when teams rotate in and out of interest and the sports fan grows older. The two-sided storage unit reinforces the "home" versus "visitor" team idea while making efficient use of space; its varied shelves accommodate assorted trophies. The cork scoreboard is big enough for posters and other memorabilia.

► CORRAL THE FRONTIER SPIRIT with lumberyard finds. This jailhouse headboard arrests attention with its shingled rooftop, shutters, and barred window. Rough-sawn planking along the wall is both evocative and functional, providing display shelves and tabletops. Crossed supports give the bed the rough and ready look of a cabin bunk.

▼ ◀ OVERHEAD ACCENT LIGHTING can energize a variety of themes, as these two bedrooms in the same house illustrate. In the castle room a ring of small, tinted lights raises the focus to the crenellations, heightening the illusion of being in a medieval tower. A dome dotted with fiber-optic lights in the other room recreates the orientation of the stars and planets on the child's birthday.

The Right Mix of Lighting

WITH GOOD LIGHTING, a child's room is safer and more pleasant to use. The room needs both overall ambient lighting and channeled task lighting. Decorative accent lights are icing on the cake.

Ceiling fixtures should illuminate the whole room, leaving no shadowy corners. Adjustable track lights can provide either ambient or task lighting, and they can be repositioned easily if the room is reorganized.

Nonglare task lighting should evenly illuminate the entire work or play area. For full coverage, ceiling lights for a desk should be as far behind as the desk is long—18 in. behind an 18-in. desk, for instance. Reading lights should beam over the reader's shoulder.

Don't forget natural light. If windows are skimpy or absent, consider adding a skylight.

CAMPING IN

▲ KIDS LOVE RUSTIC ROOMS with their promise of imaginary escape to someplace wild and adventurous. Hefty log beds, plank flooring, and paneled walls give this rugged room the allure of a house in the woods. Tucking the upper bunk against a low ceiling makes it safe as well as cozy.

◄ THE CANVAS-COVERED CEILING and raw wood molding turn a bedroom into safari digs. The fake ventilation hole, complete with faux fern, and the swinging seat add to the atmosphere—and the fun. Animal-print accessories complete the look and can be easily replaced as the child grows.

▲ EVERYTHING IS WOOD—or looks like it—in this easy-to-assemble camping room. Log wallpaper runs up to the plate shelf, which functions as a window ledge, display surface, and visual cap for the cabin space. Perching the bunkhouse bed on high crossbars makes the room feel big and open.

◄ THIS CABIN ROOM, with walls of rough-sawn plywood panels and a no-frills plywood closet, looks and lives like camp. The beds were made with real trees salvaged from construction sites. For a cozy touch, each bed has its own window and reading light.

COOL ILLUSIONS

▲ FANTASY HAS NO BOUNDS when illusion and reality merge. The gargoyle and overhead shelf fit perfectly into the painted castle wall. Rope lighting gives the shelf a dreamy glow, and small spotlights inset in the shelf bring each faux scene to life.

▶ A VERITABLE DREAM MACHINE, this room features a bed platform in the shape of a draw-bridge, which extends down from the painted castle wall. The friendly dragon, cheerful court jester, and knight in shining armor ensure a safe and pleasant sleep.

▶ SPECIAL EFFECTS open this room to the night sky. Glow-in-the-dark wallpaper runs across the ceiling and down the top foot of the walls, capping the room in stars. The faux window opens to a dramatic, looming moon. Real molding over the window intensifies the illusion while adding display space.

▲ YOU CAN ALMOST HEAR the dinosaurs roar in this wild scene. Each Masonite® behemoth is glued to a wood block so it pops right out of the landscape.

CREATIVE USE OF SPACE

▶ AROUND THE ROOM, built-in drawers, shelves, and a desktop (not shown) punctuate the wainscoting, furnishing the space without intruding on floor area. A low opening leads to a hideout that occupies surplus knee-wall space.

▼ TUCKED AGAINST THE WALL, this furniture-quality platform loft yields bonus play area over the bed and a snug shelter around it. The side columns accommodate deep shelves, and each step houses a drawer. Even the footboard is a container: One hollow post is a secret compartment, and the other holds a time capsule.

▲ ▶ THE YOUNG *STAR WARS* FAN doesn't yet need a walk-in closet, so for now his is a play annex. The metallic paint glaze promotes a sci-fi look, while foam-backed commercial carpeting makes a durable yet forgiving surface that's firm enough for rolling toys. In the bedroom, the top-only bunk bed leaves space for a seating alcove.

▼ THE HOUSE MOTIF unifies the structures in this room, and their placement and orientation organizes the space. The red-roofed, side-facing unit defines the computer center on one side, while the blue, front-facing case keeps books accessible to the desk on the other.

▲ DON'T RULE OUT THE ATTIC as bedroom territory just because the space is irregular. Sheathed in beadboard panels that contrast with surrounding walls, the chimney cone is the star of this room. Windows add light to expand the usable space; placed low to fit into the wall, they should open only partway to ensure safety.
.

► SHELVES CAPTURE otherwise underused space in the closet, keeping toys organized. With stacked rods, the closet offers plenty of accessible clothing storage for now and in the future when the child is older, taller, and has a wider range of attire.

▼ ON THE OTHER SIDE of the room a quilted fabric panel presses the wall into service as a display board over the built-in desk. The panel blends in with the funky laminate that coordinates the drawers and countertops.

SLEEPY-TIME NOOKS

▶ THIS SOFTLY LIGHTED NOOK encloses only half the bed, but that's enough to form a cozy bed niche. A poster-width wall and recessed bookshelves personalize the space. The other half of the bed doubles as a couch with bolster "arms" and built-in side tables.

◀ THE SLEEP ALCOVE and walk-in closet share a wall, tucking away both bed and belongings to leave plenty of play space. The alcove stands out as a unit, though, with its brilliant, contrasting color and wide molding at top and bottom. Inside, a reading light has pale pink glass for atmosphere.

▲ THE DRYWALL ARCHWAY forms an enchanting, skylighted niche for a child—and all her favorite toys. For visual balance, the recessed wall and stock, quarter-round windows echo the archway shape. Brackets hold the mattress in place and ease the job of bed making. There's a trundle bed underneath for guests.

◄ SOFT COLORS, a deeply angled opening, and the glow of an interior light accentuate the comfort and coziness of this bed cove. Fitted with private shelves, the niche is an exclusive retreat that preserves floor area, and the trundle bed can be rolled out for sleepovers.

BEDS MADE EASY

▶ WITH A FEW STRINGS ATTACHED, you can turn a canopy bed into a dreamy hideaway. Give it tentlike height by adding a peak or two using monofilament fishing line tacked or hooked to the ceiling. Monofilament makes a "rod" for the curtains, too.

▲ EVEN IF SPACE IS TOO TIGHT for a conventional headboard, there's room for a board like this. It was cut from Masonite, then painted and affixed to the wall with a couple of nails. The Masonite "bedside lamp" is a whimsical touch.

Making Cool Kids' Furniture

CREATING AN IMAGINATIVE BED, playhouse, or other structure for your child's room need not be daunting. Step-by-step design guides and primers on constructing wood furniture are available on the Internet and at your library. To make it even easier, an array of plans, kits, and unfinished furniture is available for purchase, as are tips and aids for decorating the furniture.

Many companies offer choices of colors and features for their kids' furniture, and some will customize products to match your needs. This bed loft/bookcase combo is an example of the products available from an Internet-based retailer. It can be ordered as a plan or as a kit of ready-to-assemble parts, either unpainted, primed, or fully painted.

▶ DESIGNED TO FIT OVER A TWIN BED, this loft arrives as a package of components to be screwed together. It comes unfinished or painted in various motifs. If you are good with tools, you can buy just the plan and build the loft yourself.

A BED MADE BETTER

An inexpensive pine bunk bed can easily be morphed into an adventure center. For strength and stability, a sheet of veneer plywood is screwed to the back of this structure. Another plywood sheet turns the upper bunk into a play platform with hinged trapdoors.

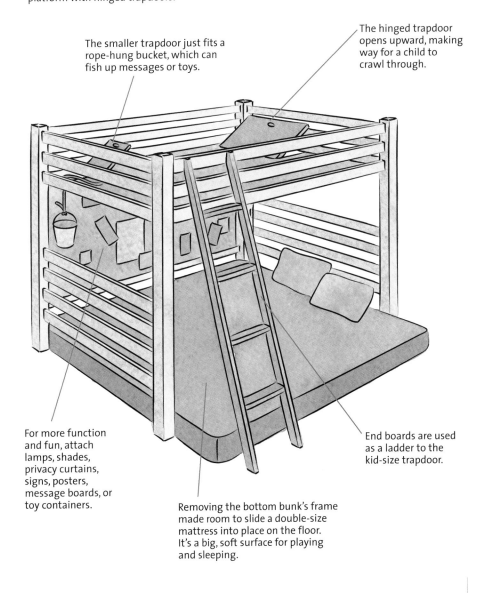

The smaller trapdoor just fits a rope-hung bucket, which can fish up messages or toys.

The hinged trapdoor opens upward, making way for a child to crawl through.

For more function and fun, attach lamps, shades, privacy curtains, signs, posters, message boards, or toy containers.

End boards are used as a ladder to the kid-size trapdoor.

Removing the bottom bunk's frame made room to slide a double-size mattress into place on the floor. It's a big, soft surface for playing and sleeping.

UP AND AROUND

▲ WITH AN UPPER BUNK/PLAY SPACE, a trundle bed, and plenty of open floor area, this masculine room is ready for a crowd of little boys. The beds are crafted from rough-hewn pine logs, while draperies hang on fishing poles. The rug was made with inexpensive carpet pieced together on site.

▶ THIS LOFT takes the playhouse idea to a new level, as it creates the illusion of a shingled house-within-a-house. It's a 5-ft. by 12-ft. room that fills surplus attic space. The glassless window openings soak in light from the skylight. The loft is carpeted and has a fiberboard wall where pictures can be tacked up.

▲ THE LOWER BUNK is a cozy haven that offers a full-size bed. But when friends come to play, everybody heads up the ladder to the "second floor," which has both a twin-size mattress under the roof and a railed passageway. The outside wall of the structure is lined with bookshelves for smart storage.

▲ TO MATCH THE PLASTER WALLS, this new closet was framed in and built using blueboard with a plaster skin coat. The doors are glass-paneled units ordered without the glass, then backed with fabric. When the room décor changes, the fabric can be changed, too. The classic built-in study unit also can be adapted as the child grows—the shelves are adjustable, and the green knobs can be replaced easily.

▲ THESE FURNITURE-QUALITY built-in cabinets give shape to the room and create a niche for the bed. The top shelves are designed for display. The others are adjustable—and removable—to hold books and toys of different sizes.

◀ WALLS TOO NARROW FOR FURNITURE can be put to use with built-in shelving. This tall unit on a sliver of wall between a window and closet houses a cabinet plus adjustable shelves. It's balanced by a matching unit on the other side of the window; the two built-ins frame the opening for the window seat.

▲ ▶ CONCEAL CD PLAYERS and television sets in enclosures that add style to the room. The "dollhouse" adorning the dresser is actually a television cabinet that's constructed of plywood and pierced with holes in the back for wiring.

ADDED DIMENSIONS

▲ THE THREE-DIMENSIONAL OBJECTS hanging on branches make this painted tree seem more real while also providing ingenious display space. The birdhouse shelf is on picture hangers; the clothesline is nailed into place.

▼ BOXED OUT just a few inches from the wall, this headboard doubles as a puppet stage. For kids with other interests, such an opening could be used for dangling fish, planets, butterflies, or airplanes.

The Real Thing

BRING NOVEL FEATURES into your child's room to create an environment where fantasies become reality—well, almost. Here are some possibilities that may enchant your child.

- Budding dancers will take great pleasure in performing at a ballet barre affixed to a mirrored wall.
- Golf aficionados can putter around at a carpeted corner mound that works like a green.
- For rising music stars, build a small stage equipped with a basic home karaoke system.
- Wannabe firefighters can stimulate their imaginations—and burn off some excess energy—by sliding down their own fire pole. Build a ladder on a nearby wall for access to the pole top.
- Kids love horses. Install a carousel-style horse that children can cherish for its beauty and ride for the fun.

▶ THIS FIRE POLE is bolted securely at the top and bottom and is surrounded with carpeting for a soft landing.

Perfect for Preteens

PRETEENS WANT TO EXPRESS who they are, but they also want to be like their friends. The result is a room that should make two statements: This is me, and I'm cool. Girls may prefer brassy rooms showcasing pop stars, or they may opt for flowery, feminine spaces. Boys may go for extreme themes, featuring sports, outer space, or science-fiction characters. In terms of storage, preteens, especially girls, will be able to fill jumbo drawers and expansive closets with clothes.

Many kids have also amassed quite a collection of memorabilia from events and activities by this age. These things merit prominent display around the room because they demonstrate defining accomplishments and experiences that lend a constant source of encouragement. A comfy corner designated for the computer—whether for work or play—is a smart addition, as is a snug bed niche where kids can be alone with their thoughts—or their headphones.

▼ FRILLS AND FEMININE COLORS are the sugar and funky details are the spice. Painted accents and playful curves in the facing make the hutch and under-window storage units cool for kids. So do the headboard and footboard, which are inverse pieces cut from the same board.

▲ DIVIDING THIS ROOM into sections organizes the space while adding personality. The sunny dormers have been turned into curtained hideaways or reading nooks. The blue ceiling defines the bedroom area and gives it a soft, feminine aura. At the other end of the room (not shown) there is a sitting area along with a computer corner.

◄ THE SINGLE-MINDEDNESS of this basketball room is a slam dunk for a preteen boy, as is the hands-on, shoot-the-hoops basket in the corner. The dashes and half balls on the wall are an inexpensive and easy-to-produce standing invitation to play.

▲ THIS COLORFUL BUILT-IN has the interest and diversity of a room full of furniture. The three sections—six-drawer bureau (not shown), central desk, and toy cabinet— have adjustable shelves on top. Green backing unifies the unit, while vertical dividers and facings add zest.

◄ A SLOPED CEILING can be used as a natural overhang, eliminating the need for canopy bedposts. Even more cool, the bed's side curtain can be unhooked to enclose a private retreat. Bump up the ceiling, and the dormer window becomes a bright, inviting study niche.

◄ GIRLS LOVE "SKY ROOMS" with blue heavens and puffy clouds. This one has extra appeal because the painted sky continues across the blinds. Rope lighting highlights this hip feature.

▼ PRETEENS CAN JAZZ UP a bedroom wall all on their own by using simple knickknack shelves, a dash of paint, and a creative arrangement of stick-on wallpaper accents.

CAPTURING EXTRA SPACE

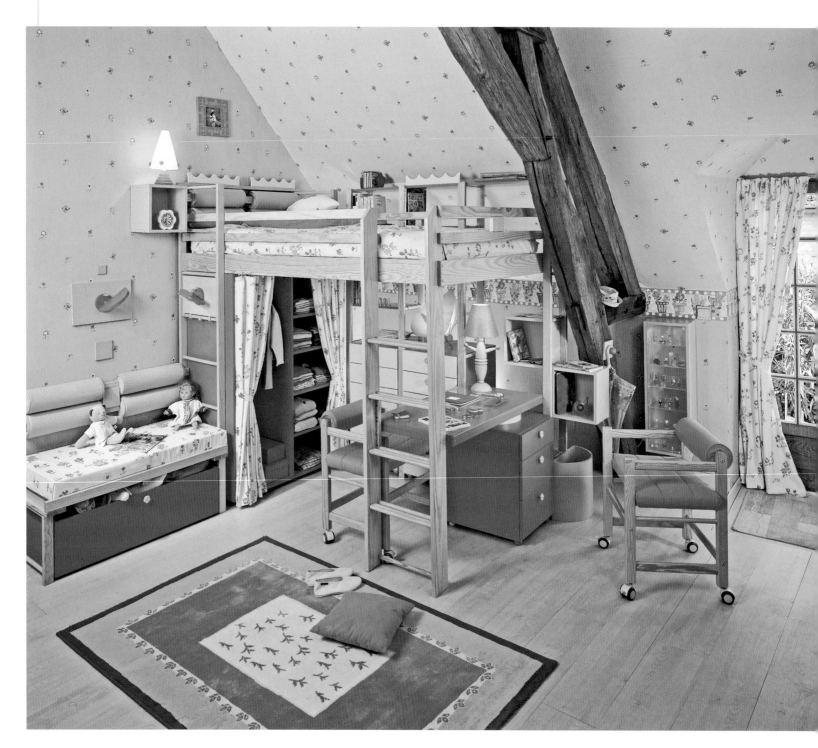

▲ ACTIVITY SPACE under a loft bed is as popular with preteens as it is with younger children, but instead of toy shelves and a play table, the preteens make use of it for clothing storage and a desk. Pulling the structure away from the wall makes room for a bureau and wall-hung shelves.

◄ ▼ THIS EFFICIENT STRUCTURE corrects the deficiencies of a small, closetless room, carving out space for a full-size bunk, a locker-look closet, and a sitting nook. On the opposite wall, corner shelves capture display space alongside the built-in cabinetry.

▶ BUILT-INS CONTRIBUTE INTEREST
and capacity to a bland, rectangular
room. The window seat and shelving
wrap around this sunny corner, taking up little room but adding consid-
erable storage. They also define an
inviting reading and relaxation zone.

◀ A TWO-SIDED STORAGE PIER doubles the storage potential while taking up only a few more inches of space than
conventional shelving. Equipped with a mirror and shelf,
this one even works as a dresser.

▶ TWO STANDARD CLOSETS may help keep things more organized than one large one. Another big advantage is that they form a niche for a dresser with walls on three sides for mirrors and bulletin boards. Provide lighting overhead or above the mirror.

Powering Up

As KIDS GROW UP, so do their electrical needs. They steadily accumulate electronic equipment, from computers and phones to audio systems, DVD players, accent lights, hair irons—you name it. Plan ahead for this surge of power usage by installing ample wiring and outlets.

Circle the room with outlets placed no more than 12 ft. apart so there's always one nearby. Run a high-capacity, CAT-5 cable to the desk area and provide at least two duplex receptacles there for the computer, monitor, and desk lamp. Install a phone jack at the desk and at least one more elsewhere in the room.

A three-way switch to the bedside lamp gives both you and your child the option of turning the light on or off at the nightstand or at the door.

◀ THIS CABINET WALL, which organized the space when it was a nursery and then a toddler's room, still does the job for the preteen who now inhabits it, holding all of her abundant belongings. Keep a few sections open for display shelves and a dressing table.

CREATIVE STANDOUTS

▼ PRETEEN BOYS like rooms that evoke adventure. This one builds on a Tom Sawyer theme, with a whitewashed fence that was apparently deserted when he was lured away by a trip to the fishing hole. The magical touch is the corner where the bed tucks inside a rail-framed cabin. The no-frills, built-in desk also has boy appeal.

▲ FINDING ADEQUATE STORAGE space is an increasing challenge as kids become more interested in clothes and accumulate other stuff. A closed unit like this wardrobe adds storage capacity without making the room too busy. In fact, the decoration makes the cabinet an important theme-setter.

Cheap Chic

CLEVER DESIGN FEATURES like those used in the room shown here are a hit with preteens and teens. Why? Because they need not cost much, they allow personal expression, and they can be accomplished by the kids themselves.

- Scour yard sales, flea markets, and secondhand stores for chairs, chests, trunks, and other furniture finds to renovate with daring paint colors and cool hardware.
- Transform old multipane windows or funky picture frames into wall mirrors by replacing the clear panes with mirror glass. Likewise, old patio doors can be re-used as closet doors, with mirrors on one side and photos, artwork, wallpaper, or paint on the other.
- Use deep-profile molding strips as shelves. Placed high on the wall, they hold decorative displays; lower shelves lend space for photos, books, and CDs. Make a fabric collage for a headboard or bulletin board. It might be a mélange of pieces from worn-out jeans or a patchwork of old team shorts and shirts.
- Shape a seating area or study by running a dowel between walls and hanging fabric from it.

▲ A STRIP OF DEEP ARCHITECTURAL MOLDING capitalizes on display space over the closet.

SPORTS STARS

▶ THIS RACE-CAR ROOM IS EXCITING and unusual, but it still has all the basics of a practical bedroom. Placed at a racy angle, the bed looks like the lead car rounding the track. The TV cabinet, finished with wheels and glossy auto paint, mimics a tool chest; gearshift knobs are a cool extra.

▼ GIRLS' ROOMS can be just as sporty as boys' rooms. White finishes make this room feminine while evoking the wintry scene where a snowboarder does her thing. The headboard wall is curved in a half pipe, and the shelving is designed as a chairlift ready to roll across the rope.

▼ OPPORTUNITIES TO CELEBRATE sports can be found on almost any surface of a kid's room. This dresser for a hockey fan turns pucks and a segmented stick into drawer pulls. The goal on the dresser top is made with mesh and wire.

▼ THE RAISED CEILING made it possible to fulfill a basketball lover's wish to shoot hoops in his room. An extra layer of felt batts soundproofs the wood floor. The under-hoop cabinet houses the TV and sound system, while rickrack shelves display autographed balls and function as a headboard.

GARDEN VARIETIES

▼ ► A GARDEN ROOM makes a cheerful environment for kids of any age but is especially attractive
to preteens because of its softness and femininity.
Vinyl or painted wood lattice, generally available
in 2-ft. by 8-ft. and 4-ft. by 8-ft. sheets, can be used
to build decorative bedposts or frame a sheltered
reading corner.

◄ BOLD FLOWERS, vibrant colors, and cool materials combine to produce groovy digs with flower power. The window cornices are made of pink vinyl—a hip alternative to more traditional materials such as wood. Big flowers—some dimensional, some painted—are scattered around to give the room energy and personality.

► INSTALLED A FEW INCHES FROM THE WALL, a trellis with soft arches unifies the built-ins and forms a bed niche. Mirrors in the dresser and vanity sections visually deepen the space and brighten the room with reflected light.

▲ ◄ SLIPPING A BED ALCOVE behind stands of real birch trees gives
this bedroom an enchanted forest feel. The alcove provides extra storage and display space with cubicle shelving and drawers at both ends
for special belongings. Fabric draped across three rods forms a
canopy, and the privacy curtains have grommet holes for durability.

▼ THE LOW, ANGLED CEILING suggests a niche; the overhead light fixture, shelves, and gently molded sideboard complete it. Though shallow, the alcove is enough to make the bed corner feel cozy and private.

▲ ▼ NIFTY NICHES are dramatized to highlight the best features of this idiosyncratic room. Dressed in bright plaid, the coves and overhangs stand out especially well because every other surface recedes with a uniform coat of leafy green.

Designed and Built by Kids

WHEN CHILDREN HELP PLAN AND IMPLEMENT their room design, they create more than a room. They build pride, identity, and a healthy sense of ownership of their unique space. Along the way, they may even learn a few life lessons.

A 10-year-old girl responded enthusiastically when invited to participate in building, furnishing, and decorating her room with loft sleeping space in the family's new house. Her parents gave her a limited budget, construction help, and advice as needed, but the decisions were her own.

She collected paint samples, opting for multiple colors inspired by her duvet cover, and the family painted the room together. She developed design ideas for a headboard and furniture, which her parents helped sketch out. After buying two stools at a yard sale, she decorated them and designed a companion table, and she even cut the pieces, assembled them, and painted the table, doing the work when her father was on hand to supervise. The lessons stuck with her, and she redesigned her room again as a teen—doing the majority of the work herself!

▶ THE EXUBERANT SPIRIT OF THE PRETEEN comes through in her loft bedroom. She covered the walls and ceiling with glowing colors, built a nightstand with dowel legs, and made the sunny particleboard headboard nailed to the bed.

▼ TWO SECONDHAND STOOLS fit the preteen's low decorating budget. She pepped them up with a rainbow paint job and tacked-on canvas seat covers that she embellished with painted swirls. A homemade corner table completes the set.

▲ FOR THIS 10-YEAR-OLD, painting every surface a different, bright color felt just right. Other personal statements include the ornamental bug she made from scraps found under her father's workbench and a message mailbox on the stairs to her sleeping loft.

Teen Domains

TEENS NEED INDEPENDENCE, and they need a place where they can assert their individuality. When planning their rooms, try to give them both. Remember: Outrageous decorating is harmless.

The more self-sufficient the room, the more a teen will like it. Choose a room location that's outside the hub of family activity. If a private bathroom is not possible, consider installing a sink and vanity in the bedroom.

Help the teen design and build a bed platform, reading nook, or other cool getaway zone. Elsewhere in the room, set up a lounge (equipped with an audio-video system, a phone, and comfortable seating) where the teen can relax with friends.

Include a homework center that has ample desktop, storage, and wiring capacity. In the closet, install shelves, deep drawers, and laundry bins; if the teen decides to use them, they'll be ready and waiting.

◄ TEENS ARE READY for big, daring ideas. A step up from car-themed rooms for younger boys, this one features a bed in a steel frame supported by heavy-duty tires and chains. The realistic computer-printed mural is a more sophisticated version of the hand-painted themes you'd expect in a boy's room.

► THIS ROOM is almost like an apartment, perfect for independence-seeking teens. There's a "living room" seating platform for friends, a "bedroom" with both niche and loft for sleeping or reading, a study space, and lots of shelves.

▲ AN ALL-IN-ONE structure makes even a small room—in fact, especially a small room—a big hit with teens. With a queen-size bed on top, this maple unit has the dimensions to accommodate a comfortable study cubicle, two banks of dresser drawers, and deep shelves.

WONDER WALL

Add jazz to a teen's room by cutting into the wall to create a cushioned alcove.

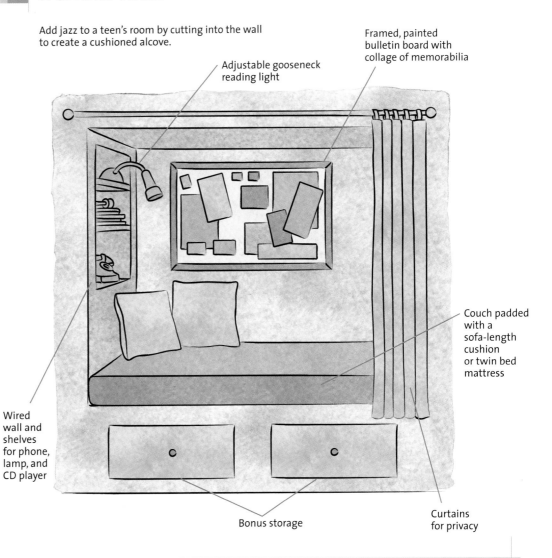

Adjustable gooseneck reading light

Framed, painted bulletin board with collage of memorabilia

Couch padded with a sofa-length cushion or twin bed mattress

Wired wall and shelves for phone, lamp, and CD player

Bonus storage

Curtains for privacy

10 Cool Ideas for Teen Rooms

THESE DIGS ARE FULL OF GOOD IDEAS, most of them generated by the teen who lives here. The room is a healthy blend of the practical and the way-out individuality most teenagers thrive on.

- The room has a separate, well-lighted study that is marked off by a short wall.
- A teen's room needs at least one show-stopping element. Here, it is the see-through fish tank on the other short wall of the study.
- The private bathroom has an extra-long counter for grooming gear.
- There's more primping space—a dressing table and a large closet with mirrored doors—outside the bathroom.
- The teen can stretch out and daydream on the long window seat. Drawers underneath hold lots of sweaters, sweatshirts, and jeans.
- She also can catch rays on her private balcony.
- Solid-core doors, carpeting, and insulated walls let her turn up the music as much as she wants.
- Parallel trim boards—at the height of the windowsill and the top of the door—hold a changing display of posters.
- Lights are on dimmer switches so they can be lowered for relaxing and listening to music.
- A curtain rod over the headboard makes it easy to change fabrics and color schemes.

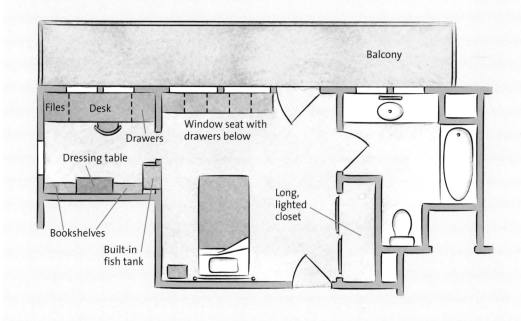

Files | Desk | Drawers | Window seat with drawers below | Balcony | Dressing table | Bookshelves | Built-in fish tank | Long, lighted closet

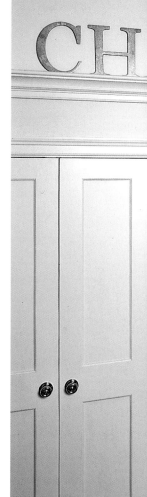

CH

▲ A 6-FT. BUMPOUT over the porch adds loft space without cutting into the room's airy vaulted ceiling area. It can be used as a sleeping place for guests or a peaceful getaway.

▲ THIS TEEN'S FOUR WISHES for her space were granted: She has a loft, a reading alcove, her favorite color scheme, and not one but two big closets. All this fits into a room that is only 13 ft. by 15 ft. The book nook, at 4 ft. by 5 ft., is big enough for a comfortable chair and two bookcases suspended from the molding.

▲ FOR A TEEN who wants her own space, nothing can top a private little house—or at least a separate wing that looks like a house.

▶ STORAGE RUNS WALL TO WALL and floor to ceiling to give this room character and make every inch count. Along with drawers and a cool collage of display shelves, this setup houses user-friendly catchall bins. When tucked under the shelving, the bed functions as a couch.

◀ THOUGH MOST TEENS tend to litter the floor with clothes, they find neater surroundings less stressful. A hamper like this conceals the mess and is so convenient that teens might actually use it; the removable bin also saves a little hassle at laundry time.

▶ CD AND DVD collections tend to stack up, like clothes, on the floor. Rickrack shelves by the computer or DVD player are a practical alternative since they keep the collections in view. They are easy to make with pine boards, some nails, and carpenter's glue.

GRADUATING TO ADULTHOOD

▶ A LOCKER ROOM THEME is fun for teens, but the quality materials and classy graphic treatment of these built-ins will hold their appeal for years. An acid wash makes the ash cabinetry look metallic; the painted walls are faux denim.

▼ THIS ROOM STRIKES a good balance between teen-friendly and adult-friendly; it has a few trendy touches, but the basic fixtures and colors are all timeless, muted, and sophisticated. The slim shelving and wraparound cabinetry is ample enough to house an evolving collection of items as the teenager grows up.

Shared Spaces

SOMETIMES SIBLINGS WANT TO BE TOGETHER, and sometimes they absolutely don't. A shared bedroom should respect that reality, encompassing common areas for play and conversation, and exclusive territory for each child to sleep, study, or simply get away.

Use furniture arrangements or low partitions to mark the boundaries between common and private zones. Shared territory may include an open area for active play, plus stations for games, crafts, and other activities involving communal toys.

Private zones should be designed to create a sense of separation from the center of activity. Strive for equity rather than sameness with these individual areas. Equip each with separate lighting, storage compartments, and display space for favorite things.

Coming up with a design motif that satisfies everyone calls for flexibility. With your kids' input, choose a family of colors, patterns, and furniture styles. Then use them to express both togetherness and each child's individuality.

◄ SMALL, SHARED ROOMS may not offer the luxury of completely separate territory for each child. This room solves the problem by radiating the built-in beds in different directions, giving each child a sense of privacy—and his own window.

► THE BOUNDARIES defining private and shared spaces are friendly but clear here. The open framework between loft beds encloses a communal window-side play center and also marks the boundary of each child's corner. Like little rooms, the corners include bed, drawers, shelving, and display space. The loft areas are separate but linked for versatility.

▲ THIS ROOM HAS A GOOD MIX of open play space, areas for group or individual activities, snug bed enclosures, and guest beds. Wainscoting, rails, and the overhanging loft enfold the beds in cozy niches, with trundles beneath. The loft works as a play area or third guest bed.

◄ THE FLOOR-TO-CEILING FOOTBOARDS on these beds function as partitions between sleeping and activity space. On one side, they shape cozy bed enclosures. On the other, they form walls for built-in desks with overhead lighting that won't disturb the kids who have turned in for the night.

TOGETHERNESS FOR FUN

► THE RAISED FLOOR and framework of overhead soffit and slim castle towers make this shared play space an enchanting destination. They also mark a useful boundary between play area and sleeping area, doing so without blocking the window.

▼ INSTEAD OF SMALLER, separate bedrooms, space was allocated in this house to give the kids one larger, shared room. The plan nets a big activity table and an indoor playground, complete with swing. Each child still has a private bed nook with drawers and display walls.

◄ ▲ **WHEN THEY FEEL** like hanging out together, the boys can shoot hoops at one end of their room or watch a video at the other. When they want some personal space, they have it—in study niches and bed alcoves.

SMALL SPACE, BIG IDEAS

▲ THIS EFFICIENT ROOM packs in lots of utility while pre-serving open play space and a bright, uncluttered look. The white closets blend into the background with fabric-lined doors that look like wall panels. For comfort and space conservation, the bunks have padded, wall-mounted "headboards." The bunk stairs contain drawers.

▲ ▼ MURPHY BEDS and a fold-down table enable this room to do double duty. At night it comfortably accommodates two beds and a shared game table. When the beds and table fold away during the day, the room becomes a play area with a decorative paneled wall.

SPECIAL CONNECTIONS

◄ WHEN SIBLINGS have adjacent rooms, there's an opportunity for playful connections. The half door that separates these sisters' rooms lends an air of intrigue while providing privacy when needed. It can be replaced with drywall or shelving if it proves to be too much togetherness when they get older.

CLOSET CONNECTION

Linking rooms with a closet corridor offers many advantages. Young children can use one room in the suite as a playroom and the other as a shared bedroom. Later they get separate, connecting bedrooms, with the option of closing the mirrored closet doors for privacy or quiet.

► A BROTHER AND SISTER can exchange toys or messages using this little pass-through in the wall between their rooms. There's a 6-in. by 10-in. door at each end, and each child has a skeleton key to lock the door for privacy.

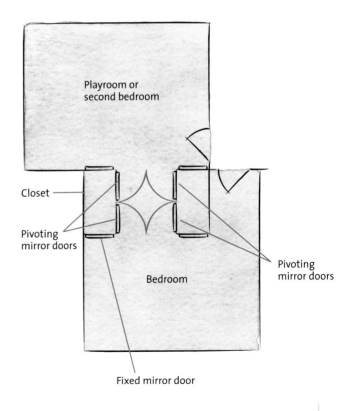

Playroom or second bedroom

Closet

Pivoting mirror doors

Pivoting mirror doors

Bedroom

Fixed mirror door

SWEET SUITES

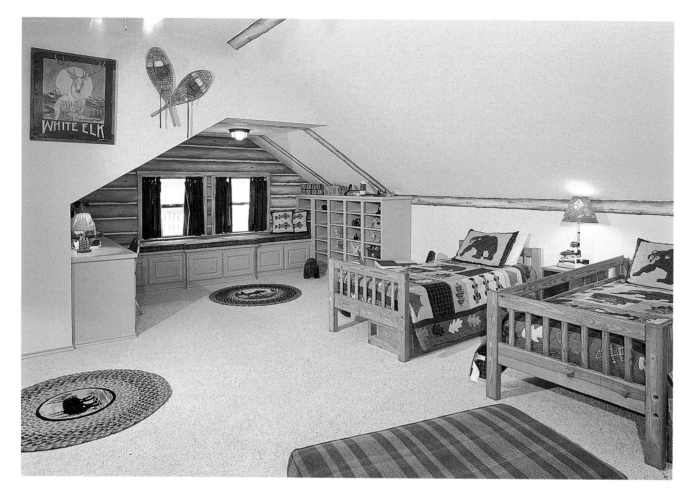

▲ EFFECTIVE ZONING turns this attic room into a versatile suite for two children. The broad, lighted window bay houses a two-person homework area, an inviting window seat with bench storage, and open shelving sized to hold see-through plastic containers for toys and computer games.

◄ THE FAUX FIREPLACE is a fun device for defining the sitting area. Recessed built-ins stow books, clothing, the television, and the audio system. With easy access to the wall from adjacent attic space, these shelves can easily be wired for conversion to a media center.

10 Cool Ideas for Kids' Suites

MULTIROOM SUITES give siblings the best of two worlds—bedrooms of their own plus common ground for play and study. Two sisters share this suite, an attic conversion that's filled with good ideas.

- The bedrooms are well separated by the shared space.
- The common area occupies an extended hall at the top of the stairs. It makes dynamic use of the space and keeps the kids' area separate but not isolated from the family area downstairs.
- Drywall partitions give each bedroom its own cool character. Walls in one room enclose a deep and dreamy bed niche.
- Partitions in the other bedroom frame a sitting nook and walk-in closets.
- The shared space is organized into zones for playing, watching TV, and studying.
- A dormer was made into a little room. The girls use it as a hideout. For sleepovers, it's the perfect place to spread out sleeping bags.
- No space is wasted. Shelves lining a narrow wall between rooms make a handy game garage.
- There's only one bathroom, but it includes a sink for each child.
- The kids have their own laundry area.
- Closets fill spare corners, giving each child storage space for her own stuff.

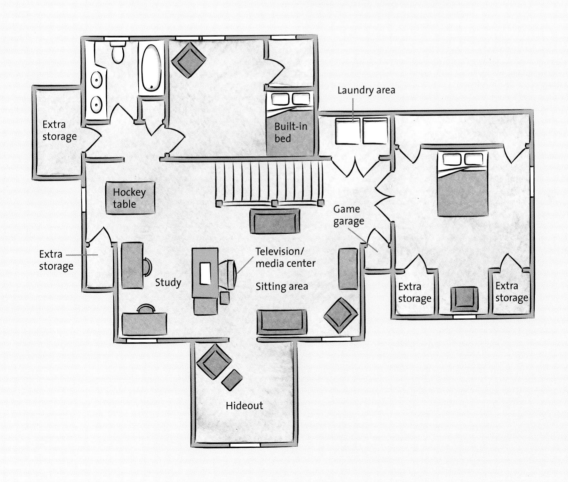

Laundry area

Extra storage

Built-in bed

Hockey table

Extra storage

Study

Television/ media center

Sitting area

Game garage

Extra storage

Extra storage

Hideout

▼ ▶ THESE COZY BED FORTS face each other so the kids can talk, but they're otherwise private and self-sufficient. Each contains a tabletop/deep display shelf under the eaves, under-bed drawers, a closet at one end, and a desk and bookshelves in the sitting area at the other. The children can keep a lookout through the portholes.

◄ ▼ **DOUBLE-SIZE BUNK BEDS** make private retreats with elbow room and enough space for a friend to sleep over. The bunks are complementary but unique, with curtains and a ladder on one, and rails and whimsical jack-and-the-beanstalk steps on the other. The three-quarter-height chair rail opens up wall space for cheery vertical stripes.

SEPARATION BY DESIGN

▼ THE CRENELLATED BUILT-IN between these beds enhances the room's castle theme and has several practical advantages, too. Most important, it separates the beds, giving each child some privacy. Also, the open shelves provide display and storage space without blocking light from the window.

◄ FOR A TODDLER a low, railed bed replaces the crib, but the cozy roof canopy remains. Lowered, the changing table has become a play table. The diaper bin now holds toys. More cabinets, some taller, contain the toddler's growing inventory of toys, books, and clothes.

◄ FOR A PRETEEN or teen, the room has a fully equipped homework alcove under a taller bed loft. Tucked under the bookshelf, the guest bed doubles as seating. Open shelving can hold a variety of things—sound system, CDs, television, books. Bins keep clothes and sports gear off the floor.

STORAGE TRANSFORMED

▼ ▶ THE BASIC ORGANIZATION of this closet system—columns of rods, shelves, and sliders—accommodates the changing needs of kids from infancy through the teen years. That's because the components are adjustable, removable, and replaceable. Young children like low bins, while preteens and teens need more drawers and shelves.

FABRIC COVERING turns an economical coated-steel unit into versatile, fun storage. In the nursery, a tent features closeable flaps that hide clutter and handy side pockets for small toys and essentials. For a toddler, the storage unit becomes a toy shelf with a playful cloth cover that's open for easy access and sports oversize side pockets.

4

Places to Play, Places to Study

Play areas and study areas have more in common than you might think. Both have a job to do, and both should be fun to use.

Every house needs territory where kids can feel free to do whatever strikes their fancy. A playroom's job is to be that kind of enabling environment. A playroom should be a friendly, lighthearted, and imaginative yet rugged place that invites kids to read, run, climb, paint, build, and make-believe. To do all that, the room needs good lighting, hardy surfaces, and an engaging mix of play stations. An expanse of open floor area, a kid-size table and seating, and ample, organized toy centers also make playrooms fun and welcoming.

Study areas, too, can be vibrant, imaginative spaces that children will enjoy using. Like playrooms, they should be comfortable and welcoming, but here the idea is to help children focus and concentrate. It's best to avoid elements that would be distracting, so separate the area from the phone, toys, and direct views into other rooms. A good homework center has excellent lighting; a comfortable, supportive chair; abundant, convenient storage for study supplies; and a desk and computer surface that are the right height for the child.

◀ A PEAKED DOORWAY creates a witty entrance to this dynamic and functional playroom. The abundant storage is a useful mix of clear-door cabinets, open shelving, drawers, and bins, allowing easy access to playthings while keeping the mess at bay. The central table, window seat, and chalkboard define various play areas, inspiring a healthy mix of activities.

Playrooms

A GREAT PLAYROOM IS A HAPPY PLAYROOM. Cozy or expansive, colorful and bright, it's a place for games, magic, make-believe, and art. Extra bedrooms, basements, unused attic space, converted walk-in closets or hallways all have the potential to become great playrooms.

Another trick to a great playroom is creating a space that's geared specifically toward your child's needs. Choose scrubbable paint or wallpaper for the walls and kid-friendly flooring that's easy to clean. Purchase furniture that's comfortable and durable, nothing you'll fret over if it gets marked up. Provide spaces for self-expression, whether by coating a wall with chalkboard paint or hanging rolls of drawing paper. Give them accessible storage and a place to put everything away. If at all possible, incorporate a little hideaway, perhaps a reading alcove, an indoor playhouse, or a portable teepee.

It also helps if you can think like a child. What did you once love? Chances are your child will enjoy much of the same.

▲ SLIDING DOORS COATED WITH A DRY-ERASE SURFACE create two separate playrooms for siblings of different ages, while a cutout in the door keeps them visually connected and allows light to filter through. A cement floor coated with high-gloss paint is perfect for this high-traffic area, and area rugs give kids a soft place to sit.

▶ A FINISHED BASEMENT becomes a full-service playroom with its separate kitchen and various activity areas. Kid- and adult-size furniture mingle easily, while plenty of accessible storage keeps the room open and spacious. A black rubber floor mat makes for easy cleaning and hides stains.

Making a Splash

APLAYROOM IS A GREAT PLACE TO EXPERIMENT WITH COLOR. Basically, anything goes. Paint every wall a different color, use bold shades you wouldn't consider using in other parts of the house, paint trim in unusual combinations, mix different colors of furniture, or go for brightly colored slipcovers. This is the place to really let your inner artist run wild.

Children respond to color. It invigorates them and stimulates their imaginations, just as it does for adults. Color in a playroom invites them to create masterpieces, invent grand adventures, and feel alive and exuberant. Just what you want in a playroom.

Color has an advantage for parents as well. Bold color and cheerful patterns disguise dirt and stains better than pale ones do, an important consideration in a playroom, where many different messy activities take place.

▲ A COLORFUL, PRIMITIVE JUNGLE MOTIF disguises clever storage and display strategies. Stuffed animals lurk behind a wooden screen, while recessed bookshelves offer additional toy storage. Flat fiberboard trees are actually display space meant for children's artwork, and vinyl flooring incorporates a game board into the décor.

▲ UNABASHED USE OF COLOR transforms this simple bedroom into a bright and cheery playroom with easy cleanup potential. The high-traffic portions of the lower walls are coated with semigloss paint, while the upper walls are painted with matte latex paint. The vivid paint job on the doors and trim helps disguise fingerprints and scuff marks.

▲ A CHILD'S VERSION OF HEAVEN, this indoor playroom provides direct access to the backyard, making it suitable for hours of play. Brightly colored accents add a playful note to this modern, soaring space, with windows overlooking the space allowing for supervision when necessary.

Flooring That Doesn't Play Around

IN HIGH-TRAFFIC AREAS LIKE A PLAYROOM, floors need to be durable and low maintenance. Instead of wood or carpet, consider cork, vinyl, linoleum, or rubber.

Cork is comfortable underfoot, comes in various stains, and can be finished with easy-to-clean urethane. Vinyl, a cinch to vacuum or mop, is available in myriad colors and designs. Linoleum, an old favorite in the kitchen, works well for the "wet side" of a playroom, where arts and crafts take place. Rubber flooring is inexpensive, sound insulated, and naturally slip-proof. And there's always the low-tech route: Use drop cloths to temporarily protect as needed.

► CREATE ACTIVITY AREAS IN LARGE SPACES to help old and young kids play together in harmony. Here, open shelving and closed storage units provide ample space for books, toys, and craft and art supplies. Two desks define space for computers and homework. Plenty of floor space allows kids of all ages to move around. If your space has stairs, like this one, consider a gate to keep toddlers safe.

▲ OPEN SHELVING SERVES AS A ROOM DIVIDER, handily separating activity zones while providing lots of storage. One side acts as a study area for older children while the other is more suitable for a toddler. A mounted ladder on a horseshoe rail allows access to items stored on high shelves.

◄ UNUSED ATTIC SPACE is easily transformed into a playroom with a bright splash of color and activity zones that conform to the lines of the room, such as the lounging area built in under the eaves. Low ceilings are balanced by kid-size furniture, making it a comfortable fit for the little ones.

◄ PLAY STATIONS pressed against the wall keep the floor clear but can be easily moved into action. The bright cabinet collage houses a rolling activity table, while art surfaces include a sliding chalkboard/display strip and a fold-back panel with corkboard on one side. Rollout toy carts are parked in color-coded garages.

▲ THE WINDOWED BULLETIN BOARD swings out from the wall, becoming a puppet theater or the wall of a make-believe house. The panel is mounted on a piano hinge, which is strong and unlikely to pinch fingers.

► THIS HOUSEBOAT PLAYHOUSE is surrounded by a harbor full of activity centers. The dock house in the background is a hideaway or puppet theater. The deck forms a curtained stage. Closets full of dress-up clothes and props flank the mirrored bench platform. Across the room are shelves of transparent toy bins and cabinets that hint at waterfront buildings.

◄ THE STURDY HOUSEBOAT, with operable shutters, steering wheel, and bell, rests on wheels so adults can move it to rearrange the room. Carpeting and fabric wall covering make a sound-insulated, cozy environment.

ART CENTRAL

▶ SPRIGHTLY IMAGES on the furniture stimulate kids to draw pictures of their own. That's easy for one or several kids to do, since the big chalkboard stretches across one wall and reaches almost to the floor. Each wall of the magical room is painted in one of the four furniture colors.

CHALKERBOARD ART WALL

A checkerboard of chalkboard and painted squares makes a decorative wall that's always changing.

The light squares are bright backdrops for framed or unframed art.

Chalkboard paint makes each black square a drawing surface.

Coated in gloss latex enamel, the light squares are easy to clean if chalk strays onto them.

Kids can "claim" their own chalkboard squares.

▲ JUST A FEW STEPS UP but sky-high in kid appeal, this reading nook has all the necessary comforts: a chaise and footrest for stretching out with a good book, natural lighting and well-placed lamps, and a soft rug. The bookcases create a sense of enclosure.

KID-SIZE GETAWAYS

▶ THIS COMPACT, cozy play corner is made all the more magical by the tiny Alice-in-Wonderland doorway that leads to adjoining play space. Kids have fun peeking through the little window and glass door; grownups can use the windows to keep an eye on things.

▼ LIGHTED, DRYWALLED, and softly carpeted, the cavity under the stairs makes an irresistible haven for kids. If there's room in such a place, add a tiny table and chairs and a shelf for books and small toys.

▶ THE SLOPED CEILING and closet walls in this attic carve out enticing play spaces. One is a cozy, sun-drenched corner; another is a tiny room—little more than a crawlspace —but the perfect secret escape for kids. The painted door adds to the sense of magic.

CHANGING AND GROWING

▶ VINYL MAKES A DURABLE PLAYROOM FLOOR, and glass turns the tabletop into an easy-care surface for art and snacks. But the room is equally appropriate for teens. The sporty patterns and colors are inviting for kids of all ages, as is the big window seat.

▼ AS THE KIDS GROW and their interests change, a room like this will keep up. The upholstered bench is good for naps and games now; its L-shape makes it a good place for older kids to hang out with friends. And the play table and toy shelves will transition into a homework center when the time comes.

TRANSFORMED SPACES

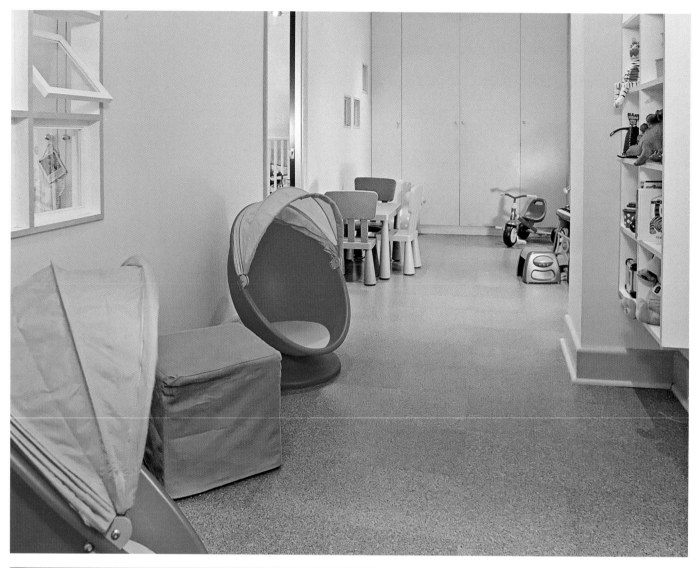

▲ A CONVERTED HALLWAY BECOMES A CHEERFUL PLAY-ROOM connected to a child's bedroom. High-density natural cork flooring is easy to care for, comfortable to play on, and sound-insulated. Cool, beautiful colors enhance the narrow space, making it seem larger, while windows between the hallway and bedroom provide light and visual flow.

◄ A FINISHED ATTIC BECOMES A HANDY ROOM for arts and crafts. The beadboard walls, covered in bright semigloss paint, make cleanup easy, as do the added sink and laminate cabinets. Window guards keep children safe while letting in natural light.

Think Outside the (Toy) Box

CHILDREN DON'T REQUIRE FANCY PLAY-ROOMS TO MAKE THEM HAPPY. Watch a child with a cardboard box and an old bed sheet and you'll see what I mean. However, children do appreciate spaces of their own—little nooks and crannies to hide in or rule over—no matter how grand or ordinary the space.

When you don't have an entire room available for play, take a look around the house and see if there are any small or awkward spaces that can be transformed. The space under a staircase can be outfitted with cushioned flooring and pillows; a built-in storage bench can become a window seat; a closet can be reworked to serve as a private hideaway.

Once you've found a spot, make it as comfortable and homey as possible. Consider including lighting, simple storage, colorful cushions or pillows, and framed artwork. It doesn't take much to transform unused space into a welcoming retreat. If you're stumped for ideas, enlist the help of your little one. He knows exactly what that closet-cum-castle needs to make it truly extraordinary!

▶ BUILT-IN STORAGE IN A HALLWAY makes for a private little hideaway. The seat was fitted with a safety hinge and transformed into a toy box. A little window keeps the area bright, while colorful pillows add a youthful, cheerful note. Attractive baskets keep building blocks corralled but accessible.

◀ A SEMIFINISHED ATTIC IS TRANSFORMED into an intimate playroom with the addition of rustic, vintage-style décor. Low storage cabinets and shelves give children autonomy, while kid-size furniture is right at home under the low ceiling. Cheerful yellow walls make the most of natural light, and a patterned area rug creates a homey feel.

Transforming an Attic

Parents with small children are constantly looking for ways to make their home live bigger. Turning an unused attic or basement into a playroom for your kids is a great way to make the most of your living space. An attic can be the perfect spot for little ones, since headroom might be limited. The low, angled ceilings provide ideal locations for kid-friendly spaces, such as a desk or bookcase built into a kneewall. Because an attic is tucked away from the main living area it also allows more freedom when painting and decorating. This is a good place to let your kids be involved in the color choice and decorating scheme.

▲ FORMERLY UNUSED ATTIC SPACE gets a makeover and becomes a bright and lively playroom with areas for floor play, theatre, and arts and crafts. Insulated flooring means children can run to their heart's content. Walls are painted in a neutral shade to make ceilings seem higher.

▲ ADDING A BUILT-IN STORAGE UNIT around the window creates a natural reading nook with space for more than one child. Underbench cabinets provide additional storage for books, while vertical shelves allow for colorful display storage.

▶ A SLIGHTLY RAISED PLATFORM creates a natural stage for performances complemented by the architectural lines of the sloped ceiling. A painted mural adds visual interest to the low wall, while hooks and treasure chests offer costume storage. A convenient wall outlet allows for additional stage lighting or music.

▲ CLOSET SPACE IS MORE FUN when masked (and used) as a vibrant puppet theatre. The painted outline forms a strong focal point for the room, and the stage curtain is simple to construct using an old sheet or other fabric secured to a spring-loaded curtain rod.

▲ WINDOWS AND SKYLIGHTS BATHE THIS ATTIC ROOM with natural light, providing a cheerful backdrop for play. Built-in storage makes use of awkward space while baskets and bins keep everything organized on the open shelves. A cheerful wall border placed at kid-level adds a playful note to this soaring space.

▶ A SMALL BEDROOM WITH HIGH CEILINGS becomes expansive with the addition of a play loft built over the bed area. An open railing provides protection without blocking light, and a secured ladder makes for safe access. A small storage closet keeps toys stowed out of sight and the bedroom below clutter-free.

▲ THIS CHARMING PLAYROOM has all the comforts of a grown-up home but scaled for the small set. Coordinated upholstery and drapes make a vivid impact, complemented by bold red accents that create a stylish, unified look. Activity zones are placed around the perimeter of the room, leaving open space for floor play.

▲ HIGH CEILINGS AND LINOLEUM FLOORING make this half of a finished basement perfect for rough-and-tumble play. Mounted plywood covered with chalkboard paint allows kids to keep score or write on the walls, a classic childhood pastime, while treated wood paneling absorbs the impact of balls without excess vibration or worry about scuffmarks.

Upstairs, Downstairs

T HE ONLY SPACE AVAILABLE for a playroom in your house may be down in the basement or up in the attic, where space is tight, headroom is limited, and light is scarce. Not to worry.

Attics and basements can make great play spaces, and their challenges frequently become opportunities to provide intimate, friendly surroundings for kids.

Here are the tricks: Tuck toy storage and play stations around the perimeter, lighting them individually and detailing them well to accentuate the variety of activities the room offers. Reserve as much open floor space as possible. In attics, use the low, angled ceilings to shape cozy, kid-size spaces. Build a dormer or pop in some roof windows to add light and height without major remodeling. In basements, light colors and good general lighting make up for the lack of windows. Carpet the walls as well as the floor, and the basement becomes a safe—and soundproof—place for kids to run around and let off steam.

◀ EVEN A SMALL DORMER or roof window improves an attic room. This one adds light, air, and a chalkboard niche. Though the window is operable, it is safe because it is high and opens only partway.

◀ THE FRESHNESS OF THE OUTDOORS infuses this bright walk-out basement play area, where structural columns are disguised as trees and overhead duct-work is enclosed in a cloudlike curved soffit. Easy-maintenance vinyl paves the art "patio." The grass-green carpet is a durable, low-pile style.

▼ THE "TOWNHOUSES" in this basement play space serve several purposes: They enliven the windowless room; offer a backdrop for city-slicker make-believe; form a whimsical environment for a lighted couch/reading niche; and provide abundant, inconspicuous cabinets, drawers, and cubbies for books and toys.

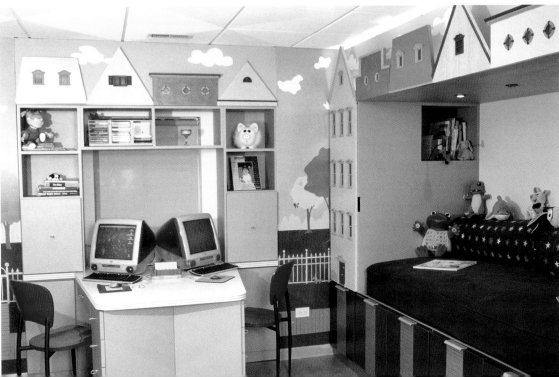

▲ WINDOWS, SKYLIGHTS, and electric lighting are well distributed around this room, leaving no murky corners and thus making every inch useful as play territory. The two-tone wall treatment with light color above de-emphasizes the angled panels and makes the room seem larger.

◄ SELF-EXPRESSION IS GIVEN FREE REIN in this playroom dominated by large boards mounted on the wall for games, display, and art. The paper roll provides an endless canvas, while labeled bins keep supplies organized and close at hand.

CLUTTER BUSTERS

Incorporating Electronics

MOST CHILDREN, FROM A VERY YOUNG AGE, WANT TO WATCH TELEVISION AND MOVIES and listen to music. Instead of letting your kids hold your entertainment devices hostage, consider giving them something of their own.

If you include a television or stereo system in your child's playroom, think about placement. You might want to put the TV on a slightly lower shelf so that it's at eye level for your children, perhaps behind doors for a less cluttered look. But keep the VCR or DVD player on a higher shelf that only you can access.

A stereo system can be hidden away behind a locked cabinet, with speakers mounted in ceiling corners to keep wires away from little ones and prevent a tangled mess. A portable CD player could be docked on a higher shelf to increase its life span and keep it out of view.

Above all, keep it safe. Kids are curious about everything and will quickly mimic your actions. Keeping electronics out of sight and reach as much as possible will alleviate some of that curiosity and the temptation to touch—safer for the kids *and* the electronics.

▶ A CUSTOMIZED BUILT-IN houses the television in this child's playroom, becoming part of the décor. The television fits tightly in the cabinet, keeping out stray objects and little hands. The VCR fits overhead behind faux drawers. Movies are stored in bottom drawers for easy selection by kids.

Super-Sizing Kid-Size Furniture

CHILDREN'S FURNITURE HAS COME A LONG WAY OVER THE YEARS. If there's an adult version, you can bet there's a child's version as well. Equipping the playroom with kids' furniture has its merits: Scaled-down pieces fit easily inside small spaces and are accessible and safe for your child.

However, the best spaces will incorporate a mix of pint-size furniture and larger-scale items that can be retained over the years. Children grow fast and you won't want to replace everything in the playroom every few years. Do consider a small table and chairs, some low storage or accessible rolling carts, and perhaps a small-scale reading chair. Balance those pieces with built-ins or large bookcases for adaptable storage and a larger loveseat, sofa, or window seat for television and movies.

Invest in the furniture that will get used the most; you'll get your money's worth out of a wooden table and chairs, but a plastic storage bin might be a better investment than a wooden toy chest soon to be outgrown. And do consider plastic blow-up furniture, such as an armchair. Its fun-factor appeals to kids, and it's a temporary, inexpensive furniture solution.

▲ A MIX OF WOOD AND OILCLOTH make this charming kid-size table and cushions durable for many years of use. Smudges and spills easily wipe off the nonstick surface, and the decorative print adds a playful note. Distressed edges keep the table kid-friendly rather than perfect looking.

▲ A SMALL WICKER VANITY topped by an oversized bulletin board easily transforms into a craft center. A vintage organizer keeps supplies handy, while a cushioned chair is easy on little knees.

▲ THE RIGHT FURNITURE CAN CREATE the feel of a playhouse within a playroom. Tucked into a corner with a windowed backdrop, the scaled-down seating, doll furniture, and a feminine table all set the stage for make-believe and entertaining playmates while an area rug serves to further separate and delineate the space.

▲ A WELL-WORN DESK becomes a creative center in a family room and is suitable for both children and adults. Grown-up supplies mingle easily with kid's supplies when stored in clear acrylic glasses. A desk mat decorated with stickers appeals to a child's aesthetics while it protects the desktop from damage.

◄ AN ALCOVE UNDER THE STAIRS gets new life as an enveloping little reading nook. Glass bricks allow for natural light, while a wall sconce is useful for nighttime reading. A fitted cushion and tons of comfy pillows make it a natural choice for a nap area as well.

Storage & Organization

WHEN THERE ARE CHILDREN AROUND, inevitably there's clutter. A path of discarded clothing, toy parts, half-eaten sandwiches...ahhh, good thing you love your kids. But while it's not realistic to expect a clutter-free zone at all times, you can save your sanity by creating storage and organization that your children can understand.

Most children don't mind pitching in and helping during cleanup—they just tend to get frustrated when they don't know what to do. You can help by making sure that everything has its place. Pegboards with illustrations, drawer dividers, labeled stacking bins, rolling storage carts, wall hooks, and shoe bags hung at child level—they're all helpful for keeping toys and clothing organized and they're accessible enough for children to use. Start early by showing them a systematic way of cleaning up and good habits will become second-nature, saving *you* a great deal of frustration down the line.

CLUTTER BUSTERS

Keep It Simple

THE EASIEST WAY TO HELP KIDS LEARN AND REMEMBER TO CLEAN UP is to keep the chore on their level, both in terms of where you place the storage bins and what they look like. If the bins are fun and recognizable, chances are good kids will actually use them. They don't need to be elaborate. Go through your closet or basement and recycle things you aren't using any longer—old hat boxes or wire baskets once used for incoming mail. A great way to get young ones excited about cleaning up is to have them first help you transform the recycled bins into kid-friendly containers with paint, old scraps of wallpaper, or fabric and ribbons.

► A CLEVER MIX OF HARD AND SOFT STORAGE OPTIONS make your child's job of cleaning up less of a chore and make use of overlooked space. If you recycle an old storage bin, be sure all edges are smooth and decorations are adhered tightly.

▲ PEGBOARDS HELP TEACH A CHILD to clean up after himself. Outfitted with hooks and pictures of what belongs on them takes all the guesswork out of where things go. It's a solution that's useful for any type of hanging object, including rackets and sports paraphernalia as they get older.

▲ FREESTANDING STORAGE UNITS and mounted shelving come together to create an attractive, organized space in a room without other options. A rolling toy cart is either a vehicle for furry friends or toy storage, depending upon your perspective. Reach-in bins are easily accessible for children, while toys requiring supervision are stored on higher shelves.

▲ THREE SEPARATE BOOKCASES CONVERGE to create one storage powerhouse. Personalized bins keep kid's items separate but accessible on lower shelves, while more delicate items are stored higher up. A small magnetic board mounted to the back of the middle bookcase is a handy place for reminders or temporary display.

▲ THIS ROLLING LAUNDRY SORTER with its deep canvas bins is perfect for holding larger and odd-shaped items, such as balls and other sports equipment. The labels, made from colored felt, leave no doubt as to what belongs in each compartment.

▼ TODDLERS ARE QUICK TO LEARN the meaning of "mine" and practice its usage regularly. Personalized storage bins cater to that idea and motivate children to put their toys where they belong. It particularly helps when children of different ages are sharing a playroom.

▲ STACKABLE STORAGE COMPONENTS form a freestanding cabinet easily tailored to individual needs, mixing open shelves with drawers and cupboards. For safety purposes, keep storage units low or mount them to the wall for added stability.

▲ AN INEXPENSIVE ROLLING CART purchased from an office supply store keeps building supplies from wreaking havoc. The clear drawers make it easy for children to identify the contents of each, limiting mix-ups of toy sets.

▲ AN OVERSIZE BOOKCASE works just as well for toy storage as it does for books. Nearly reaching the ceiling, it maximizes vertical space, while hardware mounting it to the wall keeps it from toppling forward.

Clutter Control

YOU CAN'T HAVE TOO MUCH STORAGE in a playroom. Using a mix of open and closed storage is the best strategy: Put favorite toys on shelves or in see-through bins where they can easily be seen, but keep the room from looking cluttered by enclosing other toys in labeled or color-coded cabinets, bins, baskets, and drawers. Young children can master a simple storage setup, and as kids get older, they can use a more elaborate storage system.

Store things where kids can reach them—and where they will use them. Blocks belong in bins near the floor, art supplies in divided drawers or cabinets in the craft area, dress-up clothes on a rod by a mirror or staging area. Reserve high cabinets for out-of-season equipment or for toys suitable only for older kids who share the space.

▶ SEGMENTING SHELVES into cubbyholes makes it easier for kids to organize their toys. They can reach what they want from every shelf of a unit this size. And the whole thing is on wheels; roll it around when rearranging the room or group it with others to create a storage center.

▼ VARIATIONS ON THE BASIC BOX—drawers and cabinets, shelves and pigeonholes—
hold every kind of playroom paraphernalia here. The white laminate units are
garnished with bands of open shelves that display just enough colorful toys.
Lockable upper cabinets contain toys and movies unsuitable for toddlers.

TV CABINET ALTERATION

With a few additions, you can change an inexpensive or unfinished television cabinet or armoire into a compact station for kids' activities.

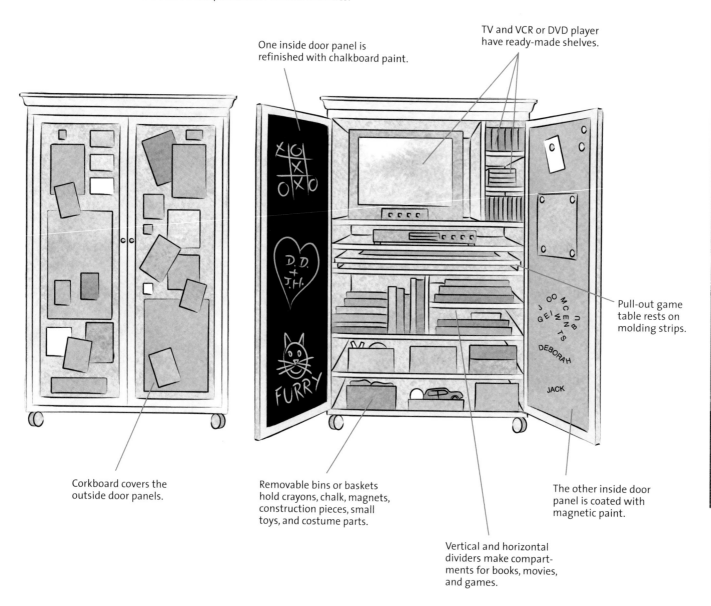

One inside door panel is refinished with chalkboard paint.

TV and VCR or DVD player have ready-made shelves.

Pull-out game table rests on molding strips.

Corkboard covers the outside door panels.

Removable bins or baskets hold crayons, chalk, magnets, construction pieces, small toys, and costume parts.

The other inside door panel is coated with magnetic paint.

Vertical and horizontal dividers make compartments for books, movies, and games.

◀ SIMPLE IN DESIGN but highly versatile, this sturdy wood wall unit has bins for books, toys, clothes, or shoes. In fact, another unit just like it is on the opposite wall of the walk-in closet. One contains toys and the other holds clothes; this simple system introduces kids to basic organizational concepts.

▶ JUST A FEW FEET of wall space is all you need for a slim rack like this. Sold as a plate rack, it works well as a place to stow or display toys, books, pictures, or collections where space is tight in kids' rooms.

STACKABLE STORAGE

▲ STACK THEM, sit on them, rearrange them—storage crates and cubes are inexpensive, strong, versatile containers that work in rooms for kids of any age. Customize the boxes with paint on the outside or inside, a fabric lining, or inserted dividers. A painted or laminated board across the top makes a smooth table surface.

◄ THESE DEEP, STACKABLE TOY BINS have wide openings but angled fronts so the contents are visible and accessible but unlikely to fall out. The dividers encourage kids to keep toys organized by type—blocks, books, games, and so on.

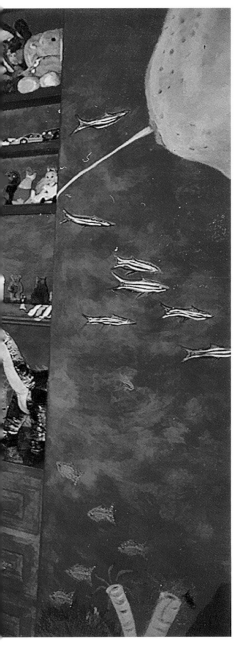

▲ THIS WALL-MOUNTED STRUCTURE positions the desktop at a standard height but hangs off the floor to preserve play space. Stained wood shelves 18 in. deep can hold speakers, computer equipment and large books. If more holes are needed for wiring, they can easily be drilled into the slim shelves.

◄ WITH A BRIGHT FINISH and a mix of drawers, cabinets, and adjustable shelves, this built-in can evolve from toy center to desk. The cabinet fits a CPU tower, and the pencil drawer is a keyboard tray. Dresser drawers can be swapped for file drawers. Glass protects the desktop.

◀ THE BUILT-IN CLOSET with overhead soffit carves out space for a cozy little study corner. Inset drawers and desk-facing shelves capitalize on space against the angled wall. Though tucked away, the corner is brightened by a window, a recessed overhead fixture, and beams from a skylight.

◄ ARCHED MOLDING and wall-hung lamps make the homework zone look important and neatly separate it from the sleeping area. The shelving and practical double-wide desk are made of furniture-look built-ins that harmonize with the trim around the room.

▼ CORNER STRUCTURES capture a lot of useful space without intruding into the room. Different-sized drawers and cabinets in this unit accommodate a variety of essentials, from CDs to files and computer equipment. The deeply recessed center section fits the TV and monitor nicely. Though they're expensive, you can't beat the customized efficiency of built-ins.

▲ CONSTRUCTING CLOSETS at both ends of the wall did more than create storage space; it formed a niche just right for a desk and comfortable chair. The arched soffit lends intimacy to the mini-study. Bookcases are workable, but shallow enough to preserve the closet cavity.

Around the House

The best homes (and the most modern) welcome children throughout the house, not just in their bedrooms, bathrooms, or designated playrooms. Comfortable family rooms replace staid, formal living rooms, emphasizing families who spend time together, even if engaged in separate activities. Formal dining rooms used only once or twice a year are scuttled in favor of eat-in kitchens or casual dining rooms used on a daily basis.

This new openness in home design reflects a realistic view of how families are actually living day-to-day. Floor plans and furnishings that embrace all members of the family are more harmonious than ones that create barriers: The goal is to produce a visual and psychic flow that offers a feeling of comfort and security.

Bridging the age gap in décor may seem daunting, but really can be quite simple. Use colors you love in durable finishes, add touches of whimsy that are playful rather than childish, and have enough storage options to keep your home from feeling like a funhouse. Of course, all ages respond to good lighting and ventilation, comfortable furniture, and open, uncluttered spaces. Finally, give everyone a little space for self-expression and individual taste and you've got a home that meets a multitude of needs.

◄ PARENTS AND CHILD ARE ABLE TO SHARE SPACE easily in this family room equipped with a kid-size portable desk suitable for coloring or other play activities. Built-in storage keeps adult possessions out of reach, while mounted shelving and decorative baskets in the alcove keep toys close at hand.

Kitchen

N O MATTER THE SIZE, THE KITCHEN TENDS to be the heart of the home. Your children will spend a lot of time here, wanting to be close to you when they're younger, peeking under pot lids when they're a little older. It's here you'll talk about your day, create memorable meals, post kids' artwork, paper the fridge with memos, and touch base with your children as they run in and out for snacks.

As the kitchen is always a high-traffic area, you can maximize its potential by creating areas in which your children can play or work without getting underfoot. A bar area, kitchen table, island, or breakfast nook all keep children away from the stove or other potentially dangerous areas while hosting casual meals, holiday activities, and homework sessions. A drawer or cabinet can serve as storage space for art or school supplies, keeping materials close at hand but out of sight. If there's room, a small alcove can be turned into a computer desk, easily accessible for both children and parents and also easy to monitor.

▲ A SMALL WORK AREA for an adult or youngster was easily created in this kitchen by taking out a pre-existing cabinet and utilizing the countertop as a desktop. Storage space was created with overhead drawers replacing under cabinet lighting and a desk drawer installed under the counter. A mounted bulletin board keeps paperwork handy.

▶ A SEPARATE KIDS' CORNER with a desk and task light built in under a kitchen cabinet puts kids where the action is but not underfoot. Art supplies are stored in the adjacent cabinet for easy access and clutter control.

▲ MEAL PREP IS A FAMILY AFFAIR with a built-in play loft over the kitchen area. Children and parents are within earshot, while kids are kept safely out from underfoot. A large open island offers another opportunity for the family to come together without getting in each other's way.

▲ LARGE OPEN WINDOWS give a spacious feeling to this kitchen-cum-family room. A comfortable sofa, television, and computer desk make this a suitable area for family members of all ages. An old wooden trunk serves as a coffee or play table for kids while meals are being prepared.

▲ A BUILT-IN BREAKFAST NOOK is perfect for casual family and kids' meals. It's also a great place for kids to hang out while meals are prepped. The storage drawers under the benches let toys and kitchen supplies co-mingle without clutter.

▲ CHILDREN LOVE TO HELP WITH MEAL PREP AND BAKING. This low countertop is ideal to accommodate little ones; enclosed sides help to contain bowls, utensils—and mess! Be sure to include child-safety locks on any low doors and drawers.

Creating a Communication Center

I F YOU'RE LIKE MOST FAMILIES, **your refrigerator door is awash in paper—to-do lists, important phone numbers, reminders, messages. It's perfectly serviceable, but eventually all those important slips of paper simply get covered by new pieces, and you're lucky if you can find the door handle.**

If you're looking for a better solution, the answer is as close as your local hardware store. Specialty paints such as chalkboard and magnetic paint allow you to create your own communication centers wherever you desire. Paint a rectangle on the wall and finish it with a store-bought frame or molding, turn a basement or pantry door into an erasable message area, or paint over an old mirror or tray. It's an easy, clutter-free solution that can free you from the tyranny of the refrigerator door.

▶ A BASEMENT DOOR treated with both chalkboard and magnetic paint serves as a handy communication center for a busy family. Artwork can be rotated and later stored or discarded; to-do lists and other everyday messages are easily erased.

Cooking with Kids

I T'S FUN FOR THE FAMILY to cook together, and it teaches kids to follow a recipe, measure accurately, and use appliances— eventually they'll be able to make those pancakes themselves and serve you breakfast! Here are some useful equipment suggestions to make cooking an enjoyable and safe experience for all:

- A sturdy pull-out step stool so kids can reach the work surface
- Low drawers for kid-sized access

- Oversized knobs on cabinets and drawers, which make it easier for kids to open them (works for older hands too!)
- Easily cleanable surfaces (stone or natural wood counters look great, but will acquire a patina of wear over time)
- A microwave placed on a lower shelf (a safe appliance for kids to use)
- A "kid's tools" drawer containing utensils that aren't too sharp but still let kids have a sense of ownership in the kitchen

▲ AS THIS MULTIFACETED space proves, the new family kitchen incorporates elements previously reserved for other rooms. Wood floors and fine carpets make their way into this space, and a comfortable wicker chair sets off a small seating area with a view. The raised ceiling above the French door has a skylight—a good way to get light into a room that often has its walls taken up with storage.

EAT-IN KITCHENS

▼ A SIMPLE, PARED-DOWN peninsula divides this informal room, which makes effective use of inexpensive materials to create the ultimate family space: kitchen and playroom all in one.

▲ A LARGE KITCHEN with many work surfaces and a pantry provides plenty of room for different family members to help prepare part of a meal for a big occasion. This island is in the center of a sea of kitchen components, including a restaurant refrigerator.

▶ A CORNERSTONE of the open floor plan, the clever use of multiple floor levels defines the boundaries of sub-spaces without resorting to walls. This well-thought-out space has a clear circulation path along the storage wall that doesn't interfere with any of the three family activity areas.

►THREE IS *NOT* A CROWD at this island eating space, where the beadboard side panels of the island form a recess for the stools. Standard counter height is 36 in., so stools should measure accordingly.

▼THIS HOMEY KITCHEN has a counter height designed for each member of the family, which allows everyone to get into the act of cooking. The deep overhang at the wooden chopping block allows you to scoop items right into a bowl or pan—quite handy. The island not only provides extra counter and workspace, it's also a compelling visual focus for the room with built-up baseboard moulding details like that of fine furniture.

◄▼A LARGE MAPLE-TOPPED ISLAND anchors the plan for this kitchen, providing a large workspace as well as an informal dining spot. A variety of materials— from steel to wood to aspen branches (legs of island, side of baskets, shelves at sink)—enliven the room, and windows over both the sink and the stove keep things light. The kitchen is open to the dining room (see the floor plan) and features a fireplace with a small seating area and a porch that has been converted to a pantry.

AN OPEN FLOOR PLAN

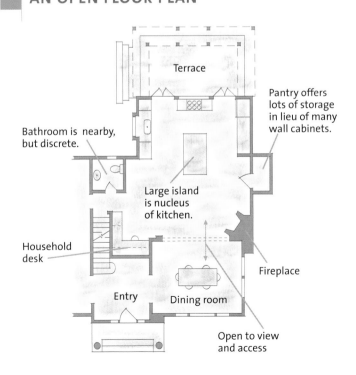

Terrace

Pantry offers lots of storage in lieu of many wall cabinets.

Bathroom is nearby, but discrete.

Large island is nucleus of kitchen.

Household desk

Fireplace

Entry

Dining room

Open to view and access

▲INTERESTING ANGLES at multiple levels give this kitchen a dynamic quality. Breakfast at the dining counter puts you at the center of family activity. One of the drawbacks of an open kitchen can be cooking odors. Here, an overhead vent at the range exhausts cooking steam and fumes.

▲THAT'S NO ISLAND, that's a continent—with six stools to accommodate the whole family. This particularly large island provides all the counter space in the kitchen, with storage on the ends and even a place to hang dishtowels. The raised section in the middle has electrical outlets, and it also shields the back of the stovetop and the sink. It's a simple layout, but one that is both effective and efficient.

►THERE IS A SCULPTURAL quality to the island in this curvaceous kitchen. The curves imply motion around the island, and the curve theme is echoed throughout the house. The island's central location within the open floor plan makes it *the* place to be during a party.

▶THIS COMPACT KITCHEN is well designed and has a comfortable look and feel. A two-pronged countertop is made up of a bead-board base and a lower section that is a kitchen table. The table can be used to roll out dough (always easier at a lower counter), and the children can reach it if they want to get involved. The peekaboo cutouts in the upper wall give a glimpse of the ceiling and beams beyond, connecting the kitchen to the rest of the house.

◀SEATING ARRANGED on two adjacent sides of an island permits diners to see one another—making it more like a table than a diner counter. This kitchen is built for entertaining, with two ovens, which allow the luxury of baking two things at once—a real timesaver.

▲ INEXPENSIVE PLASTIC laminate counters are very practical for family use—and they can be changed easily and economically if they get scorched or chipped. Plastic laminate is available in an enormous variety of colors and patterns but sometimes a simple white counter is best—it doesn't compete for attention if you want to use bright colors in other areas or put a lot of objects on display.

▶ THIS LARGE KITCHEN has two islands: one for food prep, the other for eating. The refrigerator is situated so that you can grab a drink without going through the cooking space, which a busy hostess will definitely appreciate. The contrasting white and dark-stained cabinets lend a tailored look that won't feel dated in a year or two.

◄ A BUILT-IN BREAKFAST NOOK is a
perfect spot for Sunday brunch
or for laying out bills or homework. The floor material changes
just before the top of the first
descending riser, which helps
signal the change in floor level
(and is a subtle reminder not to
move your chair back too far).

Flexible Family Kitchens

AT DIFFERENT TIMES in your family's life cycle, there will
be specific issues to consider in your kitchen setup.
Keep the following points in mind when making initial
design plans so your kitchen can flex with your family
as needed.

- **Families with young children.** Safety concerns come
  first in a room filled with appliances that cut, grind,
  and burn. Stock a cupboard or drawer with playthings—including kitchen items like pots and
  pans—that will occupy the kids while a meal is
  being prepared. Plan the circulation through the
  kitchen so that kids aren't running underfoot as you
  drain pasta into the colander. Islands help create
  good circulation—one side is the business side, the
  other is for hanging out or walking past.

- **Families with older children.** Teach older kids how to
  use appliances and utensils so they feel comfortable
  cooking on their own. Locate the microwave in a
  spot where they can reach it without climbing on a
  counter.

- **Older couples.** Ergonomics are important for getting
  things done with ease in the kitchen. Use big knobs
  with texture on appliances and cabinets for arthritic
  hands to grab. Have plenty of light, natural and otherwise. Wall cabinets should be mounted lower, or use
  a pantry in lieu of wall cabinets. Dishwashers or wall
  ovens can be mounted higher than usual within a
  custom cabinet to ease all that bending over. Avoid
  uneven handmade floor tiles.

▲ A DINING SPOT in the kitchen can be strictly utilitarian, or it can be
designed to unify the architecture and the furnishings in elegant fashion.
This table was designed as part of the architecture, with details similar to
the window screening, and a wraparound built-in bench allows additional
chairs to be pulled up. The refrigerator is situated close by for easy refills.

◀THIS INTIMATE BREAKFAST nook, with a built-in bench and loose chairs, is close to the kitchen counters to promote family time or provide a spot where guests can visit the cook. When planning built-in seating, allow room for the gentle slope at the back of the bench.

Kitchen Safety Checklist

SOME KEY CONSIDERATIONS for safety in the family kitchen:

- Locks on cabinets that contain dangerous equipment or toxic materials; these can be permanent or temporary gadgets.
- Enough electrical outlets—building codes require one every couple of feet at a counter and also at islands to avoid misuse of extension cords or cords being dragged across hot stove burners.
- A place to set hot pots when they come off the stove.
- Nonslippery flooring. Avoid little rugs that can trip you up.

▲BANQUETTES REDUCE THE AMOUNT of floor space required—no one has to move behind seated diners, and there's no need to allow clearance for chairs to pull out. This round niche has a drop-leaf table that can be enlarged for guests but saves space when not needed. The opening to the alcove is defined by the dropped beam and the stepped-down wainscot.

BOOTH REQUIREMENTS

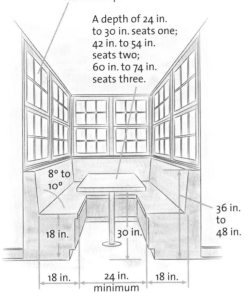

Windows make a booth feel more spacious.

A depth of 24 in. to 30 in. seats one; 42 in. to 54 in. seats two; 60 in. to 74 in. seats three.

8° to 10°

18 in.

30 in.

36 in. to 48 in.

18 in.   24 in. minimum   18 in.

30 in. per seat, 24 in. minimum

3-ft. clearance minimum, 5 ft. preferred

◄BOOTHS MAKE A GREAT design solution when space is at a premium, and they are especially good for smaller homes because you can put a booth in a space as narrow as 5 ft. wide. This intimate space is set just apart from the action in the rest of the kitchen, so it doesn't interfere with food preparation.

▲JUST LIKE AT YOUR FAVORITE DINER, in this kitchen you can pull a stool up to the counter or snuggle in a booth. The step up to the nook brings the table up to the height of the windowsill, giving the sense that the table is on grade with the landscape outside, while natural tree trunks rise up through the room, creating the playful evocation of a tree house.

▶THIS ELEGANT BOOTH boasts a slab of granite and is fastened in place on two sturdy legs. Like a proscenium arch, the beam and posts at the front of the booth define and frame it, putting the diners into a family tableau. Natural light is an important consideration for eating areas, even if the views aren't picturesque, and windows placed on all sides of the booth keep it from getting claustrophobic.

◀IN THIS THREE-SIDED BOOTH, the bench is integrated into the side of the cabinets. Benches without cushions have to be carefully detailed and dimensioned, so that they are comfortable to lean back in and the knees aren't pinched under the table. Allow 30 in. along the length of the table for each diner to be comfortable. The freestanding trestle table could be replaced if the family wants a new look later on.

ISLANDS

▶ ISLANDS COME IN MANY shapes and sizes, and this unusual one has multiple heights and surface materials. The drumlike portion has a butcher-block top for chopping and curved drawers for storage. A small but elegant granite serving area is attached, which could also double as a lower work area for little helpers.

◀ IN THIS KITCHEN, the rectangular island is the main scullery station with a double sink and adjacent dishwasher incorporated, making it a convenient dish drop-off in relation to the dining table. The peninsula (foreground) hosts the stovetop and additional prep space. The islands' shiny counters are a strong contrast against the rough-hewn beams overhead.

►FRIDAY NIGHT IS PIZZA NIGHT, but in this home that means more than calling for takeout. This "pizza island" was designed to get the whole family into the act of pizza making. Drawers and doors for trays and other equipment on both sides mean two chefs can make different pizzas simultaneously. The island is topped with a butcher-block top for rolling out the dough. Cleanup is easy with a slot that empties into a removable compost tray—complete with trash can underneath.

◄COOKING BECOMES a cooperative and communal family activity with this multipurpose island that has a cooktop, oven, storage space, and eating area all in one. It has two levels—one for cooking, one for eating. The unique chevron-shaped upper portion of the counter shields the stovetop from the diners' view.

Types of Islands

I N MANY HOMES, especially new ones, the kitchen island has taken on the multifaceted roles that the kitchen table served for years—a food preparation area, an informal eating spot, a large surface for homework and projects. Your cooking habits and the layout of your current kitchen will dictate what kind of island (if any) will add to the efficiency and convenience of your kitchen. Regardless, adding storage and outlets to any island will increase its usefulness.

Islands come in all shapes and sizes, but they generally come in the following configurations, equipped to serve numerous functions:

- Islands that simply provide a large counter surface are used solely for food preparation
- Islands that include a cooktop become a primary or secondary space for prep and cooking (it's especially useful to have two stoves if you cook or entertain a lot)
- Islands that include a cleanup sink and dishwasher and become the primary or secondary wash station (it's especially useful to have two sinks and dishwashers if you entertain a lot)
- Islands designed to accommodate seating on one or both sides, which can be used as an informal eating area, in addition to a work station

▲ THIS ISLAND IS ALL BUSINESS— no knee space for stools here. The prep sink separates the cleanup area from the cooking area and closed storage on all sides keeps things looking sleek. Stainless-steel refrigerators repel magnets, so photos, report cards, and invitations need to go elsewhere.

◀ THIS HARDWORKING ISLAND, with an end-grain chopping block and lots of storage for knives, features a microwave oven framed by a cabinet door that's been drilled with holes for ventilation. Putting the microwave down low makes it easy for the kids to use it.

THE KITCHEN AS A FAMILY HUB

◄ AS THE HUB OF FAMILY ACTIVITY, the kitchen is the hardest-working room in the house, and it pays to consider how areas can serve double duty. Here, a cozy breakfast nook is used for eating as well as making cakes and decorations for special occasions. It would serve equally well as a desk, with a phone close at hand and paperwork stowed in the nearby hutch.

▲ A KIDS' CORNER is a great way to keep little ones occupied in their own special spot, where they are under one's eye but not underfoot. A built-in desk keeps art supplies nearby. This space can be adapted later for other uses—more storage, the dog's bed, or the recycling bin.

▲ AN ADJUSTABLE-HEIGHT STOOL SWIVELS between the counter-height desk and the table-height extension of the island. The lower part of the island is good for rolling out dough, and it doubles as an eating area. The desktop can also be used as a bar or buffet when entertaining.

▲▶ THE COLORFULLY PAINTED chairs and table express the personalities of the people who sit on them in this creative kitchen full of homemade décor. In addition to the counter and table, this kitchen also has a desk/message center and a cookbook library. The stone countertop on the island overhangs at least 12 in. on the seating side—the minimum for comfort.

◄EVEN A LITTLE ANGLED COUNTER tucked into an out-of-the-way corner is better than no place at all to check your calendar. Having space for such objects, even if it's minimal, keeps the kitchen table from turning into a desk covered in clutter and papers.

Message Center Checklist

THE MESSAGE CENTER is a critical part of the family kitchen; it's the place where mail is sorted, phone messages retrieved, schedules posted, and family calendars consulted. Locate yours in an area that you have to pass by when leaving or entering the house. That way, it will be the natural spot to drop your bag or briefcase, the mail, and your car keys.

The ideal message center should have:

- some dedicated counter or desk space
- multiple outlets for the phone, answering machine, electric pencil sharpener, computer, lamp, clock
- a calendar
- phonebooks
- a bulletin board
- a chalkboard or other erasable board
- pigeonholes or cubbies for each family member
- a trash can for the junk mail
- junk drawer for tape, rubber bands, and other family flotsam and jetsom

▲THIS FAMILY'S COMMUNICATION CENTER is a French door that was reglazed with panes of porcelainized steel covered in a chalkboard finish. Each pane has a purpose—for to-do lists, shopping lists, messages, schedules, even artwork. There is space for everyone to leave messages or decorate the door.

◀IN THIS PHONE MESSAGE CENTER, the sloped counter has a lip to prevent papers from sliding off and a special cubby below for phonebooks. Above the counter, pigeonholes of varying sizes organize the mail and other items.

▶THE MESSAGE CENTER is an indispensable place in any family home. Too often, well-meaning folks plant it in a shielded, out-of-the-way location, but find that it doesn't "take." Putting the message center in a logical place along the path you automatically take when entering the house makes it far more likely that it will be used. The message center doesn't have to look makeshift or rickety; you can seamlessly incorporate it by purchasing components that match the kitchen cabinets.

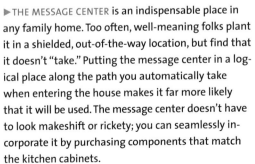

▶ IN THIS KITCHEN, the message center is combined with a space-saving idea for a breakfast table or tea for two. Cookbooks are handy for menu planning, and the TV in the corner is good for catching the morning/evening news or keeping the kids occupied while dinner's cooking.

Setting Up the Family Kitchen

- In many new homes, there's a tendency to build much larger kitchens; this can be a boon if you spend a lot of time there, but not if the work area gets spread out in the process. When this happens, the kitchen's efficiency is diminished, as you're constantly trotting back and forth between different areas. Well-designed kitchens are measured by convenience rather than square footage.

- The notion of a rigid "kitchen triangle" is challenged every day and is somewhat obsolete. There is no single geometric formula that will work for every kitchen, so design your kitchen for your particular needs and work preferences.

- Plan for multiple zones—prep, cooking, and cleanup are three different procedures, and each requires different equipment. Assembling ingredients and chopping vegetables requires access to the fridge and pantry, as well as plenty of counter space. When cooking, you need to reach spices, pans, and utensils while keeping a close eye on what's simmering on the stove. Cleanup is easiest in a scullery arrangement with a dedicated deep sink and dishwasher out of the cook's way. With multiple zones, every family member can get into the act without stepping on each other's toes.

- Set up by your kitchen according to your routine. For example, put the coffeemaker next to the cereal cabinet, and both near the toaster and the breakfast table.

- Lighting is key—a flexible combination of adequate ambient and task lighting will work for cleaning, cooking, eating, or entertaining. Choose from fluorescent, incandescent, or low-voltage lighting, and add dimmers when possible for discrete lighting or romantic midnight suppers.

- Organize your storage. The everyday things need to be most accessible—basic pots and pans, everyday dishes, silverware, lunchboxes, leftover containers. Seasonal and special-occasion items—the punch bowl, the holiday dishes, the lobster pot—can be on the periphery or even in another room. Also, match the storage to the object—a deep drawer filled with tangled cooking tools will cause massive headaches; a couple of shallow drawers is a better alternative.

▼THIS HIGHLY FUNCTIONAL message center revolves around a cabinet door that's fitted with cork for a bulletin board. Below are cubbies for mail and drawers for all the important information that collects in a home (such as appliance warranties).

▲THIS CURVY CUSTOM DESK, located alongside the pantry, proves that a workstation doesn't have to be dull or purely practical. The desktop is the perfect size for a phone, TV, and writing area, and it could even accommodate a laptop computer. The drawers create generous closed storage for all the other paraphernalia that migrates to the family hub.

◄THIS UNUSUAL BUT HANDY station marries message center and wine cooler. The cork backdrop offers a home for everything from grocery lists to kid art, while the cubby drawers above organize paper clips, rubber bands, and the like far more effectively than one big drawer. During parties, the countertop can be pressed into service as a decanting station.

◄ COMPUTERS NEED A SURPRISING amount of space, with printers, scanners, and other accessory hardware, and this kitchen devotes a corner to a mini-office. Most cabinet manufacturers are now making units that accommodate computers and other office needs and coordinate with the kitchen cabinets, as is the case here.

▼ IN THIS NOOK, the breakfast bar converts to a mail center when the cabinet doors are retracted. Pigeonholes make a handy spot for take-out menus and school schedules. The TV pulls out to keep the cook company or amuse fidgety kids waiting for dinner.

THE SMALL KITCHEN

▶MANY FAMILIES don't have the luxury of a large kitchen. This city kitchen gets it all done with an economy of space designed for efficiency of movement. You can reach the sink, stove, and refrigerator from the same spot. One uninterrupted countertop, stretching about 48 in. long, is all you really need.

◀THE OLD ADAGE "small is beautiful" applies here. This modest kitchen incorporates a blurring of the building and furnishings— the same adobe forms the shelves and alcove for the cabinets. Two tall pantries take the place of overhead cabinets. Colorful objects and artifacts and a vintage stove make this kitchen fun as well as functional.

▶THIS SMALL BUT OPEN kitchen has a casual air to it. Compact kitchen hutches flank a stove that's big enough for serious entertaining. Drop-down cabinet doors serve as countertops or prep areas, and the nearby table is another prep area. A window seat with storage drawers is just outside the kitchen, and additional storage is scattered around the room.

▼CABINETS DON'T HAVE TO BE continuous around the perimeter of a kitchen to work well. Free-standing units like these are flexible to assemble in a room that is interrupted by odd window configurations. A high-backed bench forms part of the cabinet-work as it shields the side of the island and sets off the kitchen from the dining area.

How Wide? How Tall?

IN THE 1950S, manufacturers of kitchen cabinets standardized the sizes of their products to accompany the new streamlined and modern appliances—range, refrigerator, dishwasher—that were making their way into housewives' kitchens. These standards still remain, although rules are being bent every day:

- Kitchen counters are generally 36 in. high and 24 in. or 25 in. deep.
- Allow at least 12 in. of counter space on either side of a range or cooktop.
- Allow at least 18 in. of counter space next to a refrigerator or oven (for putting down hot or heavy items).
- An overhanging counter needs to be at least 12 in. deep to be useful as a breakfast bar.
- Allow a minimum of 24 in. for each person to stand or pull up a stool at a counter.
- The space between upper and lower cabinets should be a minimum of 18 in.
- An adult needs 30 in. along a table to be comfortable while eating and to avoid knocking elbows.

◄ A SMALL COUNTRY KITCHEN in an older house makes use of limited space with tall, open shelving. The diagonally laid floor tile helps to visually expand the small room, and the center worktable doubles as a breakfast spot.

▼ WHEN THIS SPACE was renovated, a small galley kitchen got a new state-of-the-art range (hidden behind an old exterior) and a granite-topped island. A new dining alcove opened the space dramatically and incorporated storage and two more ovens.

Bathrooms

ATH TIME OFTEN VEERS BETWEEN TWO EXTREMES: You can't get kids in the tub or you can't get them out. If the former is your particular problem, it helps if the bathroom looks and feels like a fun place to be. The good news is that the bathroom, being so small, needs very little to become warm and inviting. A splash of color, a few playful accents, and you're on your way to a more peaceful experience.

If more than one child is sharing a bathroom, equality can help keep the peace. Dual sinks, cabinets, and mirrors go a long way toward giving each child a sense of ownership, as do personalized robes and towels with hooks for each occupant.

If the entire family shares a bathroom, storage becomes a key element. Adult grooming products, hairdryers, and razors must all be stored out of reach. Installing an extra medicine cabinet or a lock on existing cabinetry is a workable solution.

Individual or shared, the best bathrooms are safe, cheerful, efficient, warm, and inviting—a pleasing solution for the whole family.

▲ THESE CARS AND BUSES ARE REMOVABLE, so they're not only easy to apply but easy to remove and replace as baby grows up and tastes change. Accessories like these are widely available and versatile—they can be used individually, in collages, or in borders in any room of the home.

▶ A PLEASING MIX OF PATTERNS AND TEXTURES makes for a kid-friendly bathroom. Hooks placed low on the walls allow children to hang their own robes, while the medicine cabinet mounted high on the wall keeps its contents safe from little hands.

▲ HIGHLY CHARGED COLOR and fun patterns welcome children into this bathroom designed expressly for them. High-gloss tiles allow for easy cleanup. Patterned tiles on the floor mimic an area rug and add a burst of color, as do the painted tiles on the walls.

KIDS' BATHROOMS

▲ TWINS LOOK FORWARD TO BATH TIME with this tub designed for two. An expansive tub surround serves as play surface and storage area. The mounted safety rail inside the tub allows toddlers to get a firm grip, reducing the chances of slipping.

▲ A FORMER GUEST BATHROOM is remodeled to accommodate several small children. The long sink allows for more than one user, keeping territory disputes to a minimum. The rest of the room is vivid enough to appeal to kids but designed for easy cleanup with scrubbable walls and tile flooring.

Make It Their Own

I T's EASY TO OVERLOOK THE BATHROOM when decorating; it's a small room, less time is spent there than in other parts of the house, and it may not seem all that important overall. However, making a bathroom truly kid-friendly can make a huge difference in whether your child is happy spending time there, either taking a bath or learning to toilet-train.

Because the bathroom is small, it doesn't take much to make it a cheerful space. Colorful hooks and pegs on the wall encourage children to hang their towels or robes while a whimsical clothes hamper keeps dirty clothing off of the floor. Hand-painted tiles used as decorative accents can warm up a potentially sterile room and monogrammed or playful bath accessories such as patterned shower curtains and area rugs let kids know the bathroom is designed for them.

▲ A NARROW GALLEY just outside the kitchen is easily restyled into a kids' bathroom. The skirted tub adds a cheerful note to the small space, while a window with café curtains allows for natural light—important in such tight quarters. Kids wash their hands in the nearby kitchen.

▲ COLOR ACCENTS ADD A PLAYFUL ELEMENT to this simple bathroom. An old-fashioned claw-foot tub provides easy access for parents and easily holds more than one child, if desired. A freestanding vanity replaces bathroom cabinets, warming up the room and offering ample storage space.

SHARED BATHROOMS

▶ MIRRORS PLACED AT DIFFERENT LEVELS are accommodating to both a toddler and an older child—and are an easy solution for a bathroom shared by adults and children as well. A painted stepladder serves as storage and display space.

▼ PLAYFUL TILES ARE SCATTERED in a confetti-like pattern across a family bathroom, bridging the gap between young and old. Multiple cubbyholes and drawers provide ample storage space for the whole family. Slip-resistant textured floor tiles help prevent falls.

Childproofing the Bathroom

I T GOES WITHOUT SAYING THAT SMALL CHILDREN should be supervised in the bathroom at all times. However, you should still childproof the bathroom as if the children were going to be unsupervised. That means covering all electrical outlets and unplugging appliances not in use in addition to storing them out of reach. It also means storing medicines and cleaning supplies in locked cabinets or on very high shelves.

Beyond those basics, consider safety when choosing décor as well. Opt for slip-resistant flooring such as textured floor tiles or vinyl. If using area rugs, make sure they have nonskid backing. Rubber feet on step stools or chairs can also help prevent falls.

In the tub, grab bars help provide stability for children of all ages, as do nonskid mats or decals placed in the tub bottom.

To prevent scalding burns in the bathtub, set your water heater to a maximum of 120 degrees or install antiscald faucets. They regulate water temperature when there's a change in water pressure resulting from the toilet being flushed or faucets being turned on or off.

Finally, if very young children are using the bathroom, consider a safety latch for the toilet and always keep the seat down.

▲ STURDY FURNITURE IS IMPORTANT in a bathroom shared with a child; choose substantial pieces that aren't easily toppled. Adult grooming products are stored out of reach of small children, while the high wall ledge offers another option for storage.

◄ THERE'S ROOM ENOUGH for a family in this bathroom with its double sinks and medicine cabinets. The colorful tiles and backsplash make a bold, artistic statement in this otherwise formal, grown-up bathroom. Ventilating windows installed through the mirror further define and separate the space for double occupancy.

▼ SAFETY GETS LIGHTHEARTED with these frog-shaped nonskid decals for the tub bottom, while separate knobs are eliminated on the faucet, making it less likely for children to accidentally turn on the hot water.

▲ VIVID, SCRUBBABLE WALLPAPER and a tile backsplash disguise the messiness associated with kids' bathrooms. A small stepstool with a nonskid bottom is just the right height for little ones to stand safely at the sink.

▶ COLORED TILES are carried on in the bathtub area with alternating shades on each wall to add visual interest. A rainfall showerhead is perfect for a kids' bathroom: The gentle spray is less intimidating than a forceful stream when children are ready to graduate to showers.

Choosing Bathroom Décor

Bathrooms get notoriously messy when kids are involved. Learning to brush their teeth, washing their hands, potty training...all make upkeep a constant battle. The best options in a child's bathroom include surfaces and textiles that are easy to maintain. Scrubbable wallpaper or tile backsplashes, washable paint, tile flooring, and vinyl or brightly patterned shower curtains help disguise the daily messes until you can get to the deep cleaning.

In terms of overall décor, starting with a neutral-colored tub, sink, toilet, and cabinets will keep the bathroom from feeling dated too quickly. From there, add splashes of color in the floor or wall tiles, area rugs, window shades, walls or borders, shower curtains, and kidlike accessories. Down the road, these elements can be swapped out or updated with less expense.

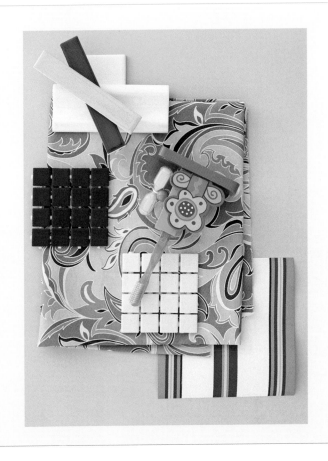

▶ ADULT PRINTS AND CHILDLIKE ACCESSORIES harmonize effortlessly when unified by color. Crisp navy and white are accented by bright bursts of yellow and lime green, an appealing palette for all age groups.

◀ WHETHER SHARED BETWEEN multiple children or children and adults, the twin sinks and shelves dividing the vanity into two sections help the room function well for more than one person. The tub/shower unit is on the opposite wall, creating zones that allow separate areas to be used at the same time.

EXTREME THEMES

▶ WHITEWASHED WOOD, a sky-blue wall, and green tile evoke a garden with a rustic picket fence, but the sponge-painted drywall clouds take the outdoor theme over the top. The clouds also serve a functional purpose by concealing can lights. Staggering the vanity height customizes the sinks for each child.

▲ THIS INDOOR "OUTHOUSE" was simple enough to construct around a regular toilet, but it lends a big sense of wit to an otherwise traditional boy's bathroom. Tucked against the wall, the private compartment is ventilated on all sides and has an overhead light. A clubhouse like this would make a great closet, too.

▲ LARGE-FORMAT WALLPAPER borders and murals create the illusion of being on board a ship. The baseboard and paneled tub surround enhance the effect by simulating the perspective of a ship's railing from the deck. The basics—a pedestal sink, white tub, and wood medicine cabinet—will transition well when these kids outgrow their seafaring days.

◄ TAKE THE PLUNGE with a total-surround design. Covering walls, ceiling, and countertop, this deep blue sea envelops the room, creating an animated, dramatic environment. The solid-surface vanity top has an integrated sink that seamlessly continues the flow of blue. Sand-colored cabinetry lends visual variety within the sea theme.

ACCENT DETAILS

▲ OTHERWISE NEUTRAL, this boy's bathroom comes
alive with forest images, from the bear tiles over the
tub to the painted moose and busy beaver. The atmosphere of adventure makes the room a delight, as does
the camouflaged door (on the opposite wall), which
connects to an adjoining room.

▶ SPARE USE OF COLOR makes this bathroom
sparkle, placing the focus on the room's
clean lines and fresh accents. The dramatic
teal vessel sink and other spots of color—
drawer pulls, ceramic tile accent strips,
mosaic floor tiles—create a friendly space
for children that will retain its appeal even
as they grow up.

Styling with Tile

A GREAT WAY to make a kid's bathroom sparkle is to use decorative ceramic tiles. They're durable, they're waterproof, and they're available in hundreds of shapes, colors, sizes, motifs, and profiles for use on floors, walls, countertops, and backsplashes.

You won't need many decorative tiles to make the design complete. Choose a theme and/or a color scheme and apply it judiciously, perhaps with a few colorful, pictorial tiles and a coordinating border of linear ceramic strips. Before buying tiles, bring home several samples to try out the sizes and colors in the bathroom.

For a more personal touch, design your own tiles. You can paint images onto existing tiles using oil-based paint over a latex-based primer-sealer. There are commercial services that will transfer your favorite images—decals, photos, kids' drawings and paintings—onto new tiles. Or you can make the tiles yourself at a crafts activity store. Be sure the decorative tiles are sized to fit with the tiles that will surround them when installed.

A tile floor or wall in one brilliant color may be all you need. The floor tile should have a nonskid finish. You can even select colored grout to offset the tiles. Thin grout lines are easiest to keep clean.

▲ A RAINBOW OF TROPICAL FISH **swims** on the tiled wall, providing a focal point of color. Floor tiles in mottled ocean shades accentuate the sea theme; their small size makes the room seem bigger.

▶ A SPRINKLING OF SPRIGHTLY ANIMALS **and insects** and a ribbon of green are all that's needed to convey a fresh riverside theme. The tiles are turned so the colorful creatures hop every which way.

DETACHABLE DECOR

▼ ▶ WALLPAPER CUTOUTS work not only on walls but also on tubs, tiles, mirrors, or any smooth surface that will not be exposed directly to high moisture. These shells and dolphins are sold pre-cut, prepasted, and ready to apply, but you can also make them from vinyl-coated, prepasted wallpaper. To remove, just wet them again.

Do-It-Yourself Wall Designs

HUNDREDS OF PATTERNS are available for youthful wallpaper, borders, and murals, but children take special joy in patterns they help to plan and create. It's never been easier to give wall designs that personal imprint.

One approach is to transfer design outlines directly onto the wall and fill them in with paint. Create the designs by drawing around puzzle pieces, cookie cutters, cutout pictures, or favorite characters traced from books. Or take your child's black-and-white line drawing to the local rubber stamp shop and have it made into a stamp to use on the wall. If you prefer ready-made stamps, let your child choose from the wide variety of whimsical art stamps available through hobby shops, rubber stamp retailers, and stamp Web sites.

Another approach is to design custom wall covering. This used to be very pricey, but digital printing has made it affordable for small, residential projects. Once scanned for conversion to a digital image, any design—including your child's art—can be transferred onto easy-to-install vinyl wall covering that comes to you in rolls. There's an hourly charge to finalize the design and prepare it for printing; the printing cost is calculated by square foot (generally about $8 a square foot or less). The larger the quantity, the lower the rate.

◄ ROLLED IN TO DELIGHT a toddler, these cars and buses can hit the road as soon as the child's interests shift, since they are removable, reusable peel-and-stick pictures. Accessories like these are widely available and versatile, as they can be used individually, in collages, or as borders.

▲ THE INTERIOR DESIGNER DREW THE LIVELY LIZARD that populates this custom-printed wallpaper, but the scene could have been drawn by the brothers who share the bathroom.

▼ FOR HIS BATHROOM, a little boy drew outlines of pictures that were then made into rubber stamps. Once the outlines were stamped onto the wall, he helped paint them in.

USING EVERY INCH

▶ PARTIAL WALLS compartmentalize the room without compromising the sense of space. The yellow wall frames the shower, and the half-height tiled wall defines the vanity area while providing some privacy for the commode. A central skylight provides even light during the day and is supplemented at night by light from ceiling and vanity fixtures.

▶ THE IRREGULAR SHAPE of the bathroom gives this vanity its own well-lighted niche. There's another vanity at the other end of the room for a sibling. The tub is open at foot and side, giving parents easy access at bath time. With a handheld shower spray, it's ready to go when the kids make the transition to showers.

10 Cool Ideas for Kids' Bathrooms

- Tuck lockers between wall studs to keep each child's bathroom gear separate, organized, and out of sight. Buy metal units or make lockers out of laminated wood. Personalize them with color, graphics, or nameplates.

- Punctuate the walls with cubbies that keep towels, toys, and toothbrushes handy.

- Paint your own tiles to add zing to the walls, floor, or tub surround.

- Sprinkle big hooks or fanciful knobs around the room at heights each child can easily reach. Color-coordinate them with drawer pulls and cabinet hardware.

- Over the sink, attach a mirror that tilts down for small children to use.

- Instead of a drawer, slide a step into the base of the vanity to give kids a boost.

- Install dual sinks, one low and one standard height. Wire the spot so that later you can replace the low sink with a compact washing machine for the kids.

- Add a brightly painted accordion door that becomes a divider as needed between vanity and tub or commode.

- Position the bathroom between two kids' bedrooms, with a doorway to each. Place one sink near each bedroom—or just outside the door in the bedroom itself.

- Cover the cabinet doors, toilet seat, and hamper with material to match the shower curtain.

Lockerlike cabinets and shelves can be inserted between wall studs.

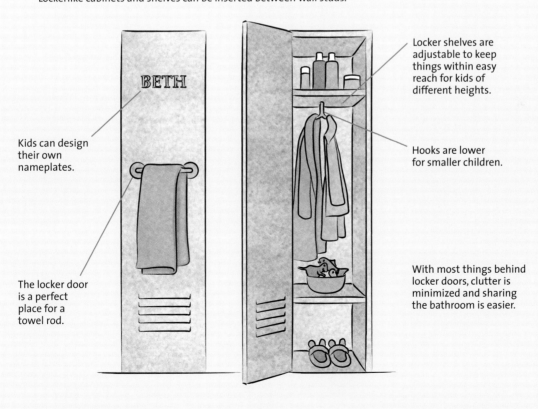

Kids can design their own nameplates.

The locker door is a perfect place for a towel rod.

Locker shelves are adjustable to keep things within easy reach for kids of different heights.

Hooks are lower for smaller children.

With most things behind locker doors, clutter is minimized and sharing the bathroom is easier.

◄ ► A BANK OF SHELVES divides the twin-sink vanity into two distinct sections, each with its own towel bar, drawers, and cabinet. The thick middle shelf in the wall unit not only matches the countertop for visual continuity; it also clearly marks the line between each child's half of the unit. The tub/shower is on an opposite wall, as far as possible from the vanity, to separate two areas that might be used at the same time.

▼ SMART CHOICES were made about what's shared and not shared in this bathroom. To avoid skirmishes over space, each child has a sink and separate storage in the vanity. Towel rods are well spaced, too, and mounted at the right height for each child. The décor is neutral enough to be universally appealing regardless of a child's age.

Kid-Safe Bathrooms

CHILDREN'S BATHROOMS should be designed to prevent falls, burns, poisoning, and the mixing of electricity and water. Nonskid flooring is essential. So are GFCI (ground-fault circuit interrupter) outlets, which help avert shocks. Choose scald-resistant faucets or set the home water heater to no more than 120°F. Stow electrical appliances out of reach and keep medicines and toxic cleaners in locked or safety-latched cabinets.

If possible, install the sink and mirror lower than standard height so kids can use them without climbing. Otherwise, provide a sturdy stool. A stool also helps small children reach the toilet, and climb in or out of the bathtub. Grab bars in the tub or shower area are always a good idea.

BONUS SPACE

▲ COUNTER SPACE is limited in this old-style bathroom, but prefinished, molded shelves solve the problem. The ventilated radiator cover adds another countertop surface and also ensures that the kids won't burn themselves.

▲ CABINETS, SHELVES, and vanity wrap like a ribbon around the bathroom, extending countertop and storage space without encroaching on floor area in this small, attic-level room. The mirror fills the wall to capitalize on the sense of additional room created by its reflection, while the roof window adds headroom and natural light. Rounding the vanity profile expands the counter area and adds a unique touch.

◀ TO MAXIMIZE both design flexibility and floor area, this bathroom uses a pedestal sink rather than a vanity. It is supplemented by a medicine cabinet with an extra shelf, and a kid-size storage bench. The wallpaper border relieves the white walls and binds the room together. As the kids get older the room can easily be repapered and furnished with different storage units.

GROWN-UP BATHS

◄ ▲ THE UNIFYING THEME here is nothing more than circles, but they're used creatively to make the bathroom both classy and fun. Kids will like the round mirror and the funky, curved vanity with off-center sink. The frosted spheres on the very grown-up frameless glass shower door look like polka dots to the kids but are just as appealing to adults.

Freewheeling Baths

KIDS IN WHEELCHAIRS can have cool bathrooms, too. The rooms need to meet certain functional requirements, but there's no limitation on style. Widen door openings and remove thresholds, raise the toilet seat, lower the sink and cabinetry, and provide knee room and plenty of circulation space. Extend windows and mirrors downward. (Consult an accessible design specialist for the particulars.) All this can be done in the context of a great-looking bathroom. Since special attention, and possibly expense, will be devoted to selection and placement of fixtures and cabinetry, it's wise to choose a design that will endure.

The rooms shown here are good examples. Designed for a young boy, the bathroom shown at bottom right provides two bathing options—a tub and a roll-in shower with handheld spray. The half wall framing the tub makes a handy ledge to hold on to. Bands of diamond-shaped tiles are bold but not juvenile; it is the rug and towels that reflect the boy's love of trucks.

A teenager uses the room shown at top right. The wall-mounted sink features a stylish, round design that's echoed by the mirror. Towels hang conveniently on low, front-facing bars. Drawers and cabinets are inset, with easy-to-reach handles. For clear access to the room, the designer used pocket doors.

▶ NOTHING IN THIS TEEN BATH looks institutional, yet it is fully accessible. The sink serves well because there's legroom underneath and a faucet that's in easy reach. The adjustable mirror angles down for use from a seated position.

▲ GOOD-LOOKING BY ANY STANDARDS, this bathroom has wide clearances for wheelchair maneuverability. In the shower, the soap dish and faucet are together for convenient use from a chair. The tub faucet is opposite the half wall so it's not in the way when the wall is used for support.

Family Spaces

▲ GROWN-UP ART AND A CHILDLIKE RUG harmonize effortlessly in this room, embracing family members of all ages. The eclectic mix of furniture is comfortable and unified by the rug's color palette. The sofa, with its vibrant cushions, is inviting and appropriately durable for this high-traffic room.

WHETHER A FINISHED BASEMENT, A GREAT ROOM, or an extra bedroom, the best family rooms are those in which all members of the family feel comfortable spending time. They're also rooms in which family members can engage in activities together, as well as pursue individual interests alongside each other.

Casual, lived-in décor, cozy seating areas, good lighting, ample storage, multiple entertainment options, and a mix of whimsy and practicality bridge the gap between age groups and make the family room one of the most appealing in the home. At its best, it's a room that holds many possibilities: a space to read, watch movies or television, play games, do homework, create art, or just talk.

A great family room serves as a haven within the home. It's where we go to relax, to get away, and to connect, all at the same time. It's a tall order for a room but a worthy goal to pursue, since the ideal home houses a family, not just separate individuals living under one roof.

▲ A BIT OF WHIMSY GOES A LONG WAY in a largely adult-styled room. Cheerful and fun, this alphabet grouping appeals to all age groups and makes the room feel more kid friendly while not coming off as a kids' room.

▲ THIS EATING AREA IS PERFECT FOR LITTLE ONES, offering room for a high chair to slide under the table, bench seating for baby as he grows up, and enough room for children to play without getting underfoot as mom gets the meal ready. Storage units with shelves and doors, plus drawers under the bench seat, offer much-needed storage for kids' stuff.

◄ A CUSHIONED BENCH is a perfect reading nook for mom and baby. This one, tucked into a stair landing, has protective railings on the side, keeping toddlers safe when they gain independence and want a place of their own to read.

SHARED SPACES

▶ BUILT-IN SHELVING AND CABI-
NETRY in a small alcove create a kids'
zone. The cabinet top serves as an
entertainment center, with space for
a small stereo system and television,
while a kid-size table and chairs
offer a place for TV viewing or arts
and crafts.

▼ SOPHISTICATION AND WHIMSY blend effortlessly in this
charming room designed for the whole family. Decorative
accents such as the umbrella lamp and muraled walls, with
their Italian vistas, are playful but not overly childish. The
elegant chandelier, sleek furniture, and rug balance but also
harmonize with the more fanciful elements.

▲ THIS L-SHAPED FAMILY ROOM hosts a variety of activity zones for all members of the family, while doubling as sleeping quarters for overnight guests (and afternoon naps). Shelving visually separates the sleeping area from the more family-friendly daybed and desk.

▲ A WOODEN DAYBED WITH HIGH SIDES is the perfect spot for family reading and cuddle time. A red wagon stylishly stores stuffed animals, and kids' artwork feels modern and fresh in a formal grouping unified by color.

▲ KEEPING TOYS CONTAINED in a family room is easy with the addition of labeled bins placed inside of a low bookcase. Because the bins are easily removed, both access and cleanup are a breeze.

ACTIVITY CENTERS

▲ YOUR CHILD WILL FEEL like she has her own part of any shared room when you enlist the aid of child-friendly boards to hang her works of art. Parents will love the creative—and inexpensive—decoration as well.

▲ PARENTS MAKE SPACE FOR KIDS in what was formerly a home office. Sliding doors with a window allow the office area to be closed off while still allowing for visual contact. Long cabinets provide ample room for toy storage and a dress-up area (the sliding doors can create a stage as well). Whimsical rugs can be moved around as desired.

▲ EXPANSIVE BUILT-IN COUNTERS are roomy enough to host the whole family in a work and play zone contained within a finished basement. Deep storage drawers accommodate plenty of toys and supplies, keeping clutter at bay. Mounted corkboard gives children space to show off their handiwork.

▲ THERE'S SPACE FOR THE WHOLE FAMILY in this comfortable room designed for solitary as well as family pursuits. Decorated storage cabinets keep games, art supplies, and toys out of sight while zones for work and study, reading or conversation, art, and floor play give everyone plenty of breathing room.

◄ A TINY ALCOVE serves as adult space in a family room. Shuttered windows offer natural light as desired and keep the area from feeling closed in. A long desk with two chairs, two lamps, and two drawers allows for double occupancy.

DEDICATED PLAY SPACES

▲ THIS UNIQUE LOFT is accessed via a climbing wall, making part of the fun getting to the play space. An interesting curved ceiling follows the roofline, and in another unusual twist, the walls are white, but the ceiling has color. The chalkboard door lets the kids get artistic without getting out a lot of supplies.

▼ THE ULTIMATE IN INDOOR PLAY! If the climate permits only a few months for swimming, then bring the pool indoors, add a spa and a slide, and all the kids in the neighborhood (adults too) will want their birthday parties here! Cedar planking lines the walls and the ceilings, creating a continuous and warming texture throughout the expansive space.

◄ RAINY DAYS are no problem if there is room inside to set up camp. Attic rooms or rooms over the garage make great playrooms. These spaces can also change over time—today's playroom is tomorrow's hobby room or gym.

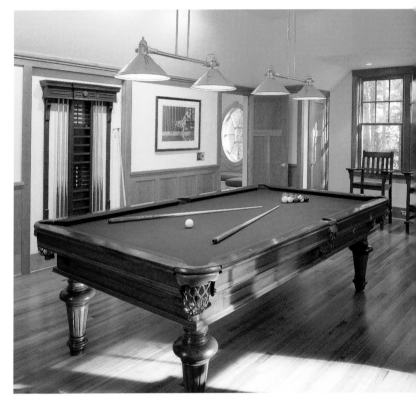

▲ HERE'S A LARGE SPACE dedicated to one pursuit. In a room of this size and configuration, a high ceiling is more comfortable, and the paneled wainscoting adds warmth. The rack holding the cues, which sits within a shallow niche framed like a doorway, adds an interesting but practical architectural element to the wall.

◀ TEENS WILL HEAD for the family game room instead of the mall with a room like this at home. The floor in this walk-out basement is on grade, so the weight of a heavy pool table is not a problem. Stone floors can be chilly in the winter, so warm things up with rugs.

▼ THIS BASEMENT has the look and feel of a pub, with pool table, deluxe bar complete with wine rack, and even a popcorn machine—it's the ultimate adult play space. A ceramic tile floor is one of many flooring choices that will work over a concrete slab base. It's durable, stylish, and easy to clean, but it's not as kind to bare feet or tumbling glasses as carpet would be.

THE LOW CEILING HEIGHT in this basement, along with the possibility of needing to reach water pipes overhead, dictated that a ceiling system of removable tiles was the best option. In this casual space subdivided into several activity zones—workout, kids' play, and bar—the tiles are both functional and aesthetically suitable to the space, particularly with the inclusion of adequate recessed lighting.

The Converted Basement

A DARK AND DANK basement can be converted into a terrific living or play space. Here are some tips on how to do it:

- Maximize ceiling heights; you want a minimum of 7 ft. to be comfortable. If ceilings are low, recessed lighting works better than hanging fixtures, which eat up even more headroom.

- Because basements tend to be somewhat damp, materials used for floors, walls, and ceilings should repel mildew. A below-ground basement is a potential flood zone in wet weather, so wall-to-wall carpeting is not always a wise selection. Better options for floor materials include vinyl tile, rubber flooring, a floating laminate wood floor (like Pergo®), or even just an area rug tossed over a concrete floor. Walls can be wood paneled or drywall, and options for the ceiling include drywall or a dropped or panelized acoustic ceiling system, which allows access to all the plumbing and electrical lines that inevitably run through a basement.

- Ventilation in warmer weather can be accomplished by an air conditioner if you don't have a walk-out basement. If a window is not available for the air conditioner, a dehumidifier will keep the air from getting musty in the summer.

- Sufficient artificial light from above is more effective than side windows, but windows should always be preserved if you're lucky enough to have them because they dispel that basement feel.

▲ THIS INDOOR BASKETBALL COURT is a far cry from the hoop nailed up on the garage, and it should keep the whole family in shape while ensuring Junior a spot on the varsity team. Wood trusses support the peaked roof of this specialty rec room, and bare stud walls provide nooks and recesses for equipment storage. The space could also be used for indoor volleyball, badminton, soccer, or garage band practice.

▶ THIS CREATIVE PLAY SPACE is a whimsical haven for kids but sophisticated enough for adults to enjoy as well. The room is unified with a graphic theme, from the shelving to the ceiling beams to the checkerboard backdrop behind the "stage." There's even a chessboard painted on the table. To add to the playful aura, wooden replicas of favorite cartoon characters, such as Pink Panther and Roadrunner, hang from the ceiling above the beams.

MULTIPURPOSE PLAY SPACES

◄ WHEN THE OWNERS OF THIS CHICAGO ROW HOUSE needed more space, they converted an adjacent rental apartment into open family space—using part as a nursery for their child and part as a family room.

▼ A ROOM WITHOUT MUCH ARCHITECTURAL CHARACTER needs a layering of furnishings to enliven it, especially if it's to be worthy of a kids' play space. This one uses built-ins, murals, layered rugs, and colorful accoutrements to raise the level of design in a boxy space. There's plenty of room for kids to stretch out and play on the floor, as well as a comfortable seating area for adults.

▲ IN THIS ADULT PLAY SPACE, dropped soffits and encased posts and beams are used to define the three regions of the room: bar, billiard, and seating areas. Glass block in the window opening lets the light in while preserving privacy and is a good option when the view is uninspiring.

► EVEN UNEXPECTED SPACES can become a spontaneous playroom, such as this area behind the stairs. It's a space where kids can see and be seen but still have a sense of privacy and freedom. An imaginative railing encases the stairway, suggesting a fort or stage and providing the backdrop for endless imaginative pursuits, while built–in storage under the landing holds lots of toys and saves the larger room from kid clutter.

Family Game Night

FAMILIES ARE SPENDING more time nesting these days, and the idea of getting the family together to play games—board games, cards, chess, or checkers—has made a comeback. All ages can participate, and there's nothing like a heated game of Monopoly to rev up the sibling rivalries and inspire conversation, recounting family lore, or spilling family secrets.

Game night will be more successful if there's a special place for it—something cozy (next to a fireplace would be ideal) with lots of comfortable seating along with a generous table for the game. If you have the space, nothing beats a dedicated game room, but game night can just as easily find a home in the corner of a living room or even around the kitchen table. The real key is making it the place that feels most like home.

▼FOR VERY YOUNG CHILDREN, basement and attic rec rooms (or playrooms in other remote areas of the house) don't work very well, because the kids want to be near their parents and require a fair amount of supervision. So partitioning off a playroom for the tykes located near the kitchen makes good sense, and it's a great way to effectively utilize a dining room that rarely sees any dinner action.

Home Entertainment

ONE ARE THE DAYS when the television was black and white and the number of channels was limited to thirteen; today a home must accommodate a wide array of electronics: TVs, stereos, VCRs, DVD players, and video and computer games. Some homes are able to devote a separate room to the "media center," which offers the luxury of closing off that space when your teenager and all her friends want to listen to music—loudly. This space might also double as the family computer room or a guest room. In smaller houses, the home entertainment components are often found in the living room.

Cabinetry, acoustics, and wiring are key concerns when designing this space, regardless of where it's located. In some families, the TVs and other gadgetry are deliberately kept behind closed cabinet or closet doors and remain a secondary focal point, while other families enjoy their media equipment out in open view, claiming all the attention. This is a design decision that will influence the furnishing and the arrangement of seating and lighting.

▼IN THIS HOUSE, the playroom, library, and home theater are all in one room. And although there is no variation in the floor or ceiling planes, the room gets some spatial variety from the bank of built-ins and fireplace that parade down the length of one wall. The large screen and speakers are built right in. The pool table at the other end of the room occupies those who don't like the movie.

◀ ▲IN THIS ELEGANT MEDIA ROOM, the cabinets are cleverly built in to tuck under the sloped ceiling. The stone chimney breast is capped by a four-paneled wood chimney portion, which gracefully arcs to match the fireplace shape while framing the mantel. When it's show time, the movie screen drops down out of a narrow channel in the ceiling and the video projector pops down from its own concealed space.

◀ ▼NO MORE WAITING in line at the multiplex—and the popcorn's much cheaper. For avid cinema buffs, it's not hard to put a theater in your own home: just buy some comfy seats and invest in a video projection setup. The brains of the operation and storage for videos and CDs can be concealed in an easily accessible closet.

Acoustics

IN ROOMS THAT HAVE too many parallel hard surfaces, sounds reverberate and make it unpleasant to enjoy music, a movie, or even conversation. Think "texture" and soften up the surfaces by adding carpets, rugs, acoustic ceiling material, and cushy seating; you'll get improved acoustics with a fuller sound and less "bounce." Locating your speakers is a balancing act between woofers and tweeters, and much of it depends on the quality of your equipment.

◄ THIS ROOM IS GEARED toward a slightly older crowd, making it the perfect teen hangout with pool table, TV, and Internet access, or a place for the adults to retire after dinner. The massive, built-up ceiling beams lend character while being an effective architectural solution to mask mechanical systems.

Media Center Checklist

WHETHER IT'S IN A FREESTANDING home entertainment center or built-in shelving and cabinets, getting the equipment set up can be frustrating if you haven't thought it through ahead of time. Important considerations include:

- Noise—ideally this area is away from the main living space and has doors and good insulation.
- Access to adequate power outlets and cable hookups.
- Pull-out shelves to reach the back of the equipment.
- Storage for videotapes and DVDs, with room to grow for the stuff that hasn't even been invented yet. Drawers with custom slots for each of these items make it easier to find the one you're looking for.
- The actual audio equipment takes up a few shelves, but your music library also has to be accommodated. Vintage LPs, cassette tapes, and CDs need to be near the audio

equipment, and depending on the size of your collection, you might need a separate closet or cabinet nearby to store the music.

- Although most electronic components today don't generate a lot of heat like their predecessors did, you should check the manufacturer's information about how much ventilation space is needed above and behind your components.
- Label the wires when setting up, so if components are moved or rearranged, you're not starting from scratch.
- Speaker locations are best decided while the walls are under construction so that you can pull wires easily. If you're "inheriting" the space, you can use the shelves and outlets that are already there, or adapt the setup to your particular system.

OPTIMAL TV VIEWING

Video technology changes constantly, but family gatherings around the tube haven't changed since "The Ed Sullivan Show." Optimal viewing distances are determined by the size of the TV and the distance and angle of the seating.

▲EVERYONE CAN WATCH his or her own program with multiple TVs and headsets in this well-equipped but understated home entertainment room, where gramophones have been wired as speakers. Flat boards on the ceiling divide it into smaller portions that relate to the wall unit at the far end, and the paneling above the window and the door ties the ceiling trim to the wainscoting.

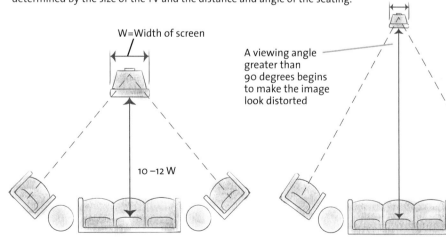

W=Width of screen

A viewing angle greater than 90 degrees begins to make the image look distorted

10 –12 W

◀ THIS BUILT-IN TELEVISION cabinet becomes an architectural feature, transferring the visual weight of the ceiling beams down to the floor. An oversize ottoman acts as both coffee table and front-row seating for those who like to lounge up close to the screen.

◀ MEDIA CABINETS tend to eat up wall space, so having the luxury of extra height for windows above permits both to share one wall. Remote-control devices can operate the windows so there's no need for a stepladder.

Mudrooms

As children get older and families grow, coats, hats, boots, balls, rackets, bats, helmets, and backpacks can start to take over a home. The best solution for this ever-expanding clutter is a mudroom, whether a formal area or just a bench, hooks, and a coat rack placed in a front or back hallway.

A well-organized mudroom not only keeps dirt from getting tracked through the house, but it also keeps gear where you can find it and discourages children from dropping clothing and sports paraphernalia on the floor.

Locker-style cubbies, hooks, storage benches, and boot racks all work to keep gear stowed attractively yet practically. Vinyl or linoleum flooring makes the indoor area easy to clean, while a sturdy doormat encourages kids to leave as much dirt outside as possible. Durable finishes, such as semigloss paint or varnished wood, help as well, making your mudroom as mud-proof as it can be.

▲ IN A SMALL ALCOVE JUST OFF THE FOYER, built-in cubbyholes with attractive baskets provide plenty of storage for each member of the family without blocking access to closets. Positioned just under a window, the ledge is a good spot for flowering plants, providing a colorful focal point.

► AN INVITING FOYER AREA does double duty as a mudroom with the addition of a storage bench and shelving that feel decorative, even as they serve a practical purpose. Overhead storage and display space is an adults-only zone while wicker baskets in the bench keep the kids' stuff where they can get to it.

▶ AN INFORMAL MUDROOM is easily created in a hallway by placing a storage bench against easy-to-clean beadboard paneling. Mounted pegs are suitable for adult-size clothing, while the whimsical star hooks are placed for child access. Sliding bins in the storage bench corral small items, and a metal pail is repurposed to hold wet umbrellas.

▼ A BACK HALLWAY IS TRANSFORMED into a cheerful mudroom for the whole family. A wide window shelve offers plenty of space to drop things off, while drawers, cabinets, and cubbies both hide and display gear as desired. Stray dirt is grabbed by a natural, easily vacuumed sisal rug.

▲ A ROOMY MUDROOM replaces a formal entryway in this family home. Individual locker-style cubbies with adjustable shelves give each family member ample storage space. Whimsical hooks are charming yet useful. Overhead cabinets help with out-of-season gear. The dark slate floor stands up to heavy-duty foot traffic.

Transform Your Entry

YOU'LL BE AMAZED AT HOW MUCH STUFF babies and children require, particularly when heading out the door. Here are some tips to help keep your entry area organized and at the ready.

- Keep your baby's diaper bag full and in the same spot so that it's easy to find.

- Use baskets or bins to hold shoes and boots.

- Install pegs or hooks for small-size jackets and hats, since they easily fall off adult-size hangers when hung.

- Provide a bench or chair for changing shoes or temporarily storing bags when you come in the door.

- If you have a closet with a door handy, hang a shoe organizer on the back and use the pockets for winter gloves.

- Stash beach gear in a canvas tote so that it's ready to go when you are. Include towels, toys, and sunscreen.

- Install a hook for keys.

▲ A ROLLING BENCH WITH STORAGE CUBBIES contributes to a make-shift mudroom in a hallway. Baking pans make handy boot trays and can be stored under the bench when not in use. Colorful canvas drawers in the shelf overhead serve as a decorative element plus they're suitable for small, easily lost items such as keys, wallets, and cell phones.

◄ BUILT-IN SHELVING AND BRACKETS turn this area, located just outside the kitchen, into an expansive mudroom. It's an easy do-it-yourself option with pre-fabricated storage units and long shelves held up by brackets. Hooks screw easily into the underside of shelving, expanding the storage options even more.

▲A FRENCH DOOR with insulating glass separates the mudroom from the living space and keeps the breeze out on a cold day. A radiator cover under the window offers a toasty seat for pulling on boots (don't obstruct the holes in a radiator cover because they let the heat out). Two rows of hanging hooks ensure that everyone in the family has easy access.

▲ A MUDROOM DOESN'T HAVE TO BE solely utilitarian; this one is used as an appealing display space as well. There can never be enough hooks for hats, and kids are more likely to hang coats on a hook than bother with a hanger. The brick floor is a good choice for a mudroom, but make sure the bricks you select are made for use as a walking surface.

◀NOT ALL HOUSES ARE LUCKY ENOUGH to have tall ceilings like this, allowing for above-closet storage that's perfect for little-used items that are reached by a stepladder. The room's colorful woodwork is shown off to its best advantage against pale walls, and with painted four-panel doors, it takes on a Scandinavian look.

Mudroom Checklist

The ideal mudroom should contain the following:

- A designated cubby for each family member to stow gear
- A bench to sit on. (It should be a minimum of 15 in. deep)
- Hooks for coats and hats
- A place to leave snowy or muddy boots
- A shoe garage for a no-shoes household
- A warm, dry spot for the dog's crate and pet food
- A shelf or hook for leaving keys and pocketbooks
- An emergency kit: flashlight, candles, and battery-run radio
- The dinner bell to call the kids in for supper
- A clock and a mirror for last-minute checks
- An umbrella stand
- As much shelf and cabinet space as can be appropriated
- Seasonal considerations, such as a mitten bin and a beach towel bin

◄ BEHOLD THE ENTRY HALL boiled down to its essence: multiple oversized hooks for speedy hangup, adjacent shelves with baskets for stowing mittens and scarves, and a narrow bench for pulling boots on and off. Staggering upper and lower rows of hooks prevents long items from concealing the hooks beneath them.

▶ CUSTOM-BUILT CUPBOARDS and cubbies above and below the bench offer abundant storage space in this stylish mudroom. The multipurpose bench is used for pulling off boots or putting down shopping bags, and it has storage for shoes or sports equipment beneath.

Outdoor Play Spaces

W HEN THEY BURST OUT OF THE HOUSE on a sunny day, kids want to play with abandon. Whether they are in the mood for adventure or make-believe, your outdoor play territory should be ready to oblige.

The yard needs at least two components—an open, grassy area for games and running around and a safe, multipurpose play structure. The location of a play structure can add to its charm. Tuck a playhouse beneath a porch overhang, perch a fort on a sentry platform, or nestle a tree house in a cluster of big trees. If the yard has a slope to roll or run down, a cluster of shrubbery to use as a getaway, or some trees to climb or hide behind, so much the better. If not, a climbable play structure with a slide, enclosures, and lookouts will do the job.

Playhouses are the stuff of childhood memories. They can be elaborate dream houses or simple shelters. As long as they are big enough for a few kids (but small enough to exclude adults) and have some furnishings, they will be popular places for children to play house, have club meetings, or spend quiet time alone.

◄ EVERY CHILD LIKES CASTLES, and this 6-ft. by 8-ft. model is packed with features that invite adventure and imaginary play—kid-size doors, a lookout tower, a climbing wall, a private courtyard, and two rooms, one of them a secret space reached through a fake fireplace.

Dynamic Playhouses

A CHILD'S PLAYHOUSE IS HIS CASTLE. It's the place where kids rule and where they feel big and important. The structure should be small enough to exclude adults but big enough to accommodate children as they grow.

Make entering the house a thrill, using tiny openings reached via a ramp, ladder, bridge, or winding pathway. Include doors and windows, cabinets and shutters, mailboxes and peepholes that open and close. Distinctive features such as trap doors, rooms behind hidden doorways, and rope-mounted message buckets make a playhouse the pride of the neighborhood.

Children often know exactly what kind of playhouse they want. They may have a specific theme, location, or features in mind. Ask them to share their wish list, perhaps by drawing a sketch. Implement their ideas while using materials and colors that complement your house, and you'll have an imaginative structure that's as attractive to use as it is to behold.

▼ AS CHILDREN GO UP THE GANG-PLANK to this castlelike structure, they move into an imaginary world filled with play possibilities, from the lookout tower above to the "jail" with trapdoor access and rear exit. The decorative back of the porch bench is a bed backboard.

Retooling Existing Buildings

YOU MAY ALREADY HAVE THE MAKINGS of a play structure on your property. Reinvent a toolshed or garden hut as a playhouse by giving it a Dutch door, a low window or two, and flooring of wood, vinyl, or indoor-outdoor carpet.

Extra garage space may work as well. Wall off and insulate an area on the side of the garage, adding a little door and window for access and ventilation. If there's an unused attic corner overhead, install a ladder to give the garage "house" a loft.

The area under a sufficiently raised deck is fertile territory for a hideout enclosed with wood fencing. If space allows, add a platform or segment the playhouse into rooms connected by small doorways or peepholes.

INSIDE THE COTTAGE the magic continues. Stained faux framing and white-painted, textured drywall mimic the look of an old-fashioned timber-frame house. The pine floor looks enchantingly rustic, too. The house has a nonworking stone fireplace and kid-size tables and chairs with tree-branch legs.

MINIATURIZE ANY TYPE of structure, and it can become a magical play-house. This English cottage, just 230 sq. ft., has the diamond-pane windows, arch-top wood doors, rolled eaves, and steam-bent shingles of a fairy-tale house in the woods. The walls are stucco; the chimney is stucco stone.

MUCH OF THE ALLURE of this four-room outpost is that its location, afloat on a slope in a wooded corner, speaks of adventure and secrecy. The deep overhang, high-railed balcony, and multiple entries—including "girls only" and "boys only" doors—equip the rustic cabin for clubhouse and play scenarios.

JUST LIKE HOME

▲ THIS TIDY LITTLE HOUSE with Dutch door and operable windows is irresistible for children. The covered front porch is just right for a couple of kid-size rocking chairs. The porch light and indoor fixtures make the house a fun place for parties or summer sleepovers.

◄ IT'S FUN TO PLAY HOUSE in this kitchen, which has real cabinets for cookware and dishes, a pretend refrigerator, and a fake stove with burners and big, turnable control knobs. The laminate flooring is durable, low-maintenance, and splinter-free.

▶ WITH OPERABLE WINDOWS and both front and back doors, this luxurious little place feels like a real house. Window bays add versatility to interior space. Pretty enough to dress up the backyard, the house also has its own fenced and gated yard for play space or a pint-size garden.

◀ THE CHARM of this garden getaway is that it is a tiny version of the main house, complete with picket fence and window boxes. The two-tiered interior is simple and open—big enough for young children to play or older kids to hang out.

UP, UP, AND AWAY

▼ BIG, CLUSTERED TREES make a broad base for this double-decker tree house. Trunks function as ladder rails at the base and as defining shapes to climb or play around within the house and on the deck. Another ladder, located inside the house, leads to the deck. Operable shutters protect the house from the elements.

▲ A FANCIFUL PAINT JOB raises the appeal of this elevated playhouse sky-high. Mounted on stilts, the plywood structure perches tantalizingly under overhanging branches, beckoning kids to climb up, peek out, and slide down.

▼ TO PROTECT THE GRAND, overhanging trees, this post-mounted house was built amid them but not attached to them. Designed as a preteen retreat, it has a steep, "adult-unfriendly" access ladder, a kid-size porch, and cable railings that ensure safety without blocking views.

► EXPOSED STUDS and sheathing give this house the rustic appeal of a clubhouse; the white walls and big, screened windows make it homey and comfortable. The preteen "homeowner" participated in the final stages of construction, specified the colors, and chose the furnishings and decor.

Active Outdoor Adventure

CHILDREN NEED TO TEST THEIR PHYSICAL LIMITS. Outside is the best place for this joyful experimentation, and an outdoor play structure should let kids stretch their skills in a safe, engaging environment.

The best structures stimulate kids' imaginations with appealing themes and varied play zones. Yet they are neutral enough to accommodate many solo and group activities and a wide range of make-believe worlds.

Create a self-contained play center or graft one onto trees or hills. Include multiple levels and platforms that become mini-destinations entered and exited via kid-size ladders, slides, ramps, bridges, grab bars, even climbing walls and zip lines. Incorporate a tunnel or steering wheel for toddlers, a climbing rope and tire swing for school-age children.

For soft landings, erect the structure over a 12-in.-deep bed of wood mulch or chips, sand, rubber mulch, or a surface of synthetic turf or rubber matting. If possible, position the structure where you can supervise from the house.

▼ KIDS PLAY OUT THEIR DREAMS of being firefighters—or just burn off extra energy—in this 9-ft. by 9-ft. brick and cedar firehouse. They can climb a ladder and slide down a fire pole inside or ring the tower bell and shoot down the spiral slide. A weather-proof coating covers the rooftop deck.

Station Nº 1½

◄ SCREENED PLATFORMS branch out from this big tree, creating a draw for kids of all ages. Young children like the swings, the slide (made of polyurethane-coated signboard), and the cedar fort with climbing rope shooting out a trapdoor. Teens climb the wraparound tree stairs and relax in the fort.

◀ THOUGH PATCHED together with scrap lumber and inexpensive parts, this house is packed with play power—a plywood up-ramp, a slide, a crane rigged with rope-and-pulley bucket that's operated from inside the house, and a 20-ft. drain hose capped with plastic funnels for whispering messages. An acrylic topper turns the chimney into a skylight.

Decks and Patios

DECKS AND PATIOS expand the footprint of the home to offer a new arena for family fun. If there's an in-ground pool, hot tub, or barbecue area, you're likely to find a deck or patio surrounding it.

Sitting close to the ground but not exactly upon it, decks and patios come in all shapes and sizes, from simple platform decks to expansive multilevel deck-and-patio combinations. The perimeter can take any shape and will be determined by the lay of the land, conforming to the topography by following the natural contours of slopes and plantings.

In addition to the traditional wood and stone building materials, you have the opportunity to incorporate a broad range of ingredients into the mix—water, views, rocks, plantings—when designing a deck or patio. These outdoor spaces need to be equipped and furnished like other rooms of the house, but here the elements are a bit more playful, encompassing umbrellas, grills, built-ins, and fountains, to name a few.

▼ GIANT STEPPING STONES made of rainbow pink sandstone from Canada lead the way to this backyard pool. The ground slopes away around the pool, but retaining walls made of irregular cuts of the same stone keep things on the level. Mirroring the design of the owners' Victorian carriage house, the pool cabana provides a place to change, stow gear, and even serve blender drinks at the outdoor counter.

▲EXTRA-LONG BENCHES and lots of uncluttered square footage ensure that this deck gets used often for family gatherings and entertaining. The deck gently inhabits the landscape, making room for several trees to rise up through it, so as not to sacrifice the shade.

◀A WELL-THOUGHT DECK area can establish different activity zones. Here, the gazebo is one destination; it can host a campout or be a refuge from the bugs. Another destination is the deck itself, with built-in benches that offer additional seating for a crowd. The hot tub is used year round, so keep it close to the back door for cold-weather tubbing.

DECKS

▲ STURDY RAILINGS are needed for a second-floor deck, and although the building code may require only a 36-in.-high railing, you may want it to be a bit higher when the deck is more than a few feet off the ground like this one.

▶ THE TRANSITION FROM built landscape (house) to natural landscape (yard) happens in several stages here, proceeding from the enclosed space of the living room to the open-sided, roofed space of the porch, to the floored space of the deck, and finally to the lawn. The house braces the deck on two sides, so it's not just an afterthought tacked on one end.

▶ON THIS COASTAL TERRACE, the surrounding wrought-iron railings have been fashioned into storybook figures that add a whimsical element to what is already a splendid view. Birdwatchers can sit on hand-hewn furniture and enjoy an uninterrupted vista.

▼SITING IS IMPORTANT in all exterior design, and climate and sun angles should inform your choices. The midday sun is too hot to enjoy in some latitudes, so umbrellas or leafy trees are must-haves for poolside dining.

BRICK PATTERNS FOR PATIOS

Running bond

Basket weave

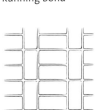

Ladder weave

Herringbone

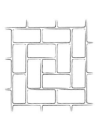

Whorling square

Lighthearted Landscaping

EVERY INCH OF THE YARD IS GAME for kids at play; bring out the fun with whimsical landscape elements. Create magical destinations by strategically placing bowers or paved patches in secret corners. Or frame small clearings with bushes, trelliswork, or wood fencing, and dot the encircling walls with tiny openings for "spying" or sending secret messages through.

Getting to these covert places can be half the adventure. Map a route that follows a winding path, perhaps one that slips under overhanging trelliswork and crosses a little bridge spanning an ivied depression, little pond, or rocky outcropping.

Fanciful features can be subtle enough to fit into sophisticated designs. Insert tiles of varied colors and shapes into the backyard terrace, forming creative patterns that double as games. Or use do-it-yourself paving pieces displaying your family's handprints, footprints, names, or artwork carved into tiles and then glazed.

▶ THIS HOPSCOTCH PATIO is a picturesque, easy-care landscape enhancement and a fun play surface. The cast concrete stepping stones, purchased at a home and garden store, are set in mortar over a concrete slab.

Sunken Treasure

JUST AS EVERY CHILD WANTS A BACKYARD TRAMPO-
LINE, every parent worries that his or her
kids will fall off the trampoline and get
hurt. Here's a solution: a trampoline at
ground level. This standard 12-ft.-diameter
trampoline nests in a 3-ft.-deep cavity with
grass all around and a buffer of surrounding
hay bales for good measure. Children love
jumping on the trampoline alone or with
friends, and a parent can jump aboard too,
delighting a small child by causing him or
her to rocket into the air.

The pit for this trampoline is reinforced
with a retaining wall of corrugated metal
and 12 symmetrically placed steel pipes. A
homemade jig pivoting on a central pipe was
used to make sure the pipes were positioned
properly. Compacted soil pads the space
between wall and tramp, while a redwood
rim forms a smooth and attractive border.

In areas with high precipitation, it's a good
idea to install a central drain under the trampoline or an underground pipe that funnels
water to a lower part of the yard.

▲ THIS TRAMPOLINE IS A POPULAR GATHERING PLACE where kids can enjoy a casual bounce or two, or work on
their gymnastics. The hay bales form a protective wall for young children and a launching platform for
older ones.

Resources

Associations

The American Institute of Architects
1735 New York Avenue, NW
Washington, DC 20006
202-626-7300
www.aia.org

American Society of Interior Designers (ASID)
608 Massachusetts Avenue NE
Washington, DC 20002
Main web site: www.asid.org
For names of ASID members in your area, go to the referral web site: www.interiors.org

American Society of Landscape Architects
636 Eye Street, NW
Washington, DC 20001
202-898-2444
www.asla.org

Associated Landscape Contractors of America (ALCA)
150 Elden Street, Suite 270
Herndon, VA 20170
(800) 395-ALCA
www.alca.org
Members are a mix of design/build contractors, installation, landscape maintenance, and interior landscape firms.

Association of Professional Landscape Designers
1924 North Second Street
Harrisburg, PA 17102
717-238-9780
www.apld.org

International Play Equipment Manufacturers Association
1924 North Second Street
Harrisburg, PA 17102
888-944-7362
www.ipema.org

Master Pools Guild
9601 Gayton Road, Suite 101
Richmond, VA 23233
800-392-3044
www.masterpoolsguild.com

National Association of Home Builders
1201 15th Street, NW
Washington, DC 20005
800-368-5242
www.nahb.org

National Association of the Remodeling Industry (NARI)
4900 Seminary Road, #3210
Alexandria, VA 22311
(800) 611-6274
www.nari.org
List of contractors.

National Kitchen & Bath Association
687 Willow Grove Street
Hackettstown, NJ 07840
www.nkba.com
Members are kitchen and bath design specialists. The web site has projects, remodeling tips, and it lists design guidelines.

National Spa & Pool Institute
2111 Eisenhower Avenue
Alexandria, VA 22314
703-838-0083
www.nspi.org

National Association of Professional Organizers
www.napo.net

Manufacturers & Suppliers

Babybox.com
www.babybox.com

Charley's Greenhouse & Garden
17979 State Route 536
Mount Vernon, WA 98273
800-322-4707
www.charleysgreenhouse.com
greenhouses and gardening
supplies

Childlife
55 Whitney Street
Holliston, MA 01746
508-429-4639
www.childlife.com
backyard play structures

The Container Store
888-266-8246
www.containerstore.com
Online custom planning, storage
solutions, and products

Decorating Den
800-DEC-DENS
www.decoratingden.com

Frontgate
800-626-6488
www.frontgate.com
outdoor living and home
furnishings

Glidden Paint
800-454-3336
www.glidden.com
Ideas, products, and color
consulting

The Land of Nod
www.thelandofnod.com

Laneventure
P. O. Box 849
Conover, NC 28613
800-235-3558
www.laneventure.com
outdoor furniture, kitchens, and
fireplaces

Netkidswear.com
www.netkidswear.com

Pacific Yurts Inc.
77456 Highway 99 South
Cottage Grove, OR 97424
541-942-9435
www.yurts.com

Posh Tots
www.poshtots.com

Putting Greens Direct
866-743-4653
www.puttinggreensdirect.com
residential putting greens

Serena & Lily
415-389-1089
www.serenaandlily.com
Contemporary bedding and fabric for nurseries and kids' rooms

Smith & Hawken
800-940-1170
www.smithandhawken.com
patio and garden furnishings

Velux America, Inc.
www.veluxusa.com

WallCandy Arts
212-367-8872
www.wallcandyarts.com
Peel and stick wall art for kids'
rooms

The Warm Biscuit Bedding
Company
800-231-4231
www.warmbiscuit.com
Bedding, furniture, fabric, and
accessories

Warmly Yours
1400 E. Lake Cook Road Ste. 140
Buffalo Grove, IL 60089
800-875-5285
www.warmlyyours.com
radiant floor heating

WaterSports Products
619-271-2750
www.watersportsproducts.com
outdoor games including oversized chess sets

Additional Reading

American Baby magazine
www.americanbaby.com

Architecture in the Garden by
James Van Sweden. Random
House, 2002.

Child magazine
www.child.com

*Colors for Your Every Mood:
Discover Your True Decorating
Colors* by Leatrice Eiseman,
Capital Books, 2000

Creating the Not So Big House
by Sarah Susanka. The Taunton
Press, 2000.

The Essential Garden Book
by Terence Conran and Dan
Pearson. Crown Publishers,
Inc., 1998.

*Fine Gardening Design Guides:
Landscaping Your Home.* The
Taunton Press, Inc., 2001.

Fine Homebuilding magazine.
This is also a good resource,
especially its special annual issues
on *Houses* and *Kitchens and
Baths.*

Home: A Short History of an Idea
by Witold Rybczynski. Viking
Penguin, 1986.
This book has become a classic,
discussing the evolution of the
idea of home, from medieval
times to the present.

Home Storage Idea Book by
Joanne Keller Bouknight. The
Taunton Press, 2002.

John Brookes Garden Masterclass
by John Brookes. Dorling
Kindersley, 2002.

The Landscape Makeover Book
by Sara Jane von Trapp. The
Taunton Press, Inc., 2000.

Y. Lai; Edie Twining, Monastero & Associates, Inc., Cambridge, MA; p. 168: Photo courtesy Sageworks.com (Sageworks Decorative Painting); Drawing by Brenda Gartman, Gartman Custom Works of Art, Shelburne, VT; p. 169: Drawing by Laura Birns, ASID, Laura Birns Design, Del Mar, CA; p. 170: (top) © Bradley Olman; Bonnie Pressley, Allied ASID, Benbrook, TX, Interiors by Decorating Den; (bottom) © Virtually There; Karen Brown, Allied ASID, Karen Brown Interiors, Inc., Tampa, FL; p. 171 (top) Interior design by Position By Design, Doug Handel photographer; (bottom) © Michael Pennello Photography; Mary C. Strickland and Bea Hopkins, Residential Design Concepts LLC, Virginia Beach, VA ; p.172: (top) © Tria Giovan; (bottom) © Ken Gutmaker; p. 173: © Peter Krupenye; The Office of Carol J.W. Kurth AIA, Bedford, NY; p.174: (top right) © Robert Perron; (bottom right) Photo courtesy Karie B. Calhoun & Joyce Cerato; p.175: (top) © Tria Giovan; (bottom) © Norman McGrath; p. 176: (top) Photo © 2005 Carolyn L. Bates/www.carolynbates.com ; (bottom) Photo © Ricardo Moncada; Victoria Benatar, Architect; p. 177: (top) Photo © Chipper Hatter; (bottom) Photo © Barry Halkin, Barry Halkin Architectural Photography; Neil K. Johnson, Architect, AIA; pp. 178-179: Photos © GetDecorating.com; p. 180: (left) Photo courtesy Velux-America, Inc.; (right) Photo © Jane Frederick,

Architect; p. 181: (top) Photo © Tria Giovan; (bottom) Photo © Rob Karosis; p. 182: Photo courtesy Velux-America Inc.; p183: (top) © Greg Premru; LDa Architects, Cambridge, MA; (bottom) Photo courtesy Michelle Rohrer-Lauer, Michelle's Interiors Ltd., Photo by Barry Dowe Photography; p. 184: Photo courtesy Velux-America Inc.; p. 185: (top) Photo courtesy Velux-America Inc.; (bottom) © Tria Giovan; p. 186: (top) Photos © Brian Vanden Brink; Design by Perry Dean Rogers & Partners, 617-423-0100; (bottom left) Photo © Wendell T. Webber; Alla Kazovsky, Architect, Kids StudioWorks; (bottom right) Photo courtesy The Warm Biscuit Bedding Co., www.warmbiscuit.com; p. 187: Photo © Mark Samu; Design by Lucianna Samu Design; p. 188: (top) Photo © Wendell T. Webber; (bottom) Photo © Tim Street-Porter; p. 189: (top) Photo © Tim Street-Porter; (bottom) Photo © Mark Samu; Design by Correia Design; p.190: (left) Photo courtesy The Warm Biscuit Bedding Co., www.warmbiscuit.com; (right) Photo © Tim Street-Porter; p. 191: (top left) Photo courtesy Levels of Discovery; (top right) Photo © Lisa Romerein; (bottom) Photo © Tim Street-Porter; pp. 192-194: Photos © Wendell T. Webber; p. 195: Photo © Tim Street-Porter; p. 196: Photo courtesy Maine Cottage, Dennis Welsh, photographer; p. 197: © John Gillan; Marc-Michaels Interior Design, Winter Park, FL; p. 199: (left) © Sargent 2002; Marc-Michaels Interior

Design, Winter Park, FL; (right) © John Umberger; Cynthia Florence Interiors, Allied ASID, Atlanta, GA ; p.200: (top) Photo courtesy York Wallcoverings; (bottom) Photo courtesy The Land of Nod; p. 201: (top right)© 2002 Michael C. Snell; Jolayne Lyon Hawver ASID, Design Consultants Inc., Greg Inkmann, Topeka, KS; (top left) © James Carrier; Steven House, AIA, House + House Architects, San Francisco, CA; (bottom left) Photo courtesy Michelle Rohrer-Lauer, Michelle's Interiors Ltd., Photo by Barry Dowe Photography; p. 202: (top) Photo courtesy Maine Cottage, Dennis Welsh, photographer; (bottom) © The Gallick Corporation, Design/Build Contractor, Photo by Woody Cady Photography.; p. 203: © Kathy Detwiler, Designer: Jennifer Mitchell, Jennifer Mitchell Design, Grosse Pointe Farms, MI; p. 204: Photo courtesy Sageworks.com (Sageworks Decorative Painting); Terry Terry Design, Dallas, TX; p. 205: (top) © Elisabeth Groh; Barbara E. Hafften Allied ASID, Barbara Hafften Interior Design, Chisago City, MN, Brian Amundson, Mother Hubbards Cupboards, Hager City, WI (bottom) Photo courtesy Contemporary Woodcrafts, Inc., Cabinets designed and manufactured by Contemporary Woodcrafts, Inc., Springfield, VA; www.cwcabinet.com; p.206: Photo courtesy Pi Smith; Smith & Vansant Architects, Norwich, VT; p. 207: (top left) © Phillip H. Ennis

Photography; Ferguson, Shamamian & Rattner, LLP, New York, NY (bottom left) Photo courtesy Michelle Rohrer-Lauer, Michelle's Interiors Ltd. Photo by Doug Hoffman, Studio West Ltd; (right) © Phillip H. Ennis Photography; Ferguson, Shamamian & Rattner, LLP, New York, NY

Chapter 5
p. 208: Photo by Charles Bickford, © The Taunton Press, Inc.; p. 210: (top) Photo by Karen Tanaka, © The Taunton Press, Inc.; (bottom) Photo by Charles Miller, © The Taunton Press, Inc.; p. 211: Photo by Charles Miller, © The Taunton Press, Inc.; p. 212: Photo by Andy Engel, © The Taunton Press, Inc.; p. 213: Photos by Charles Miller, © The Taunton Press, Inc.; Design (bottom photo) by Jim Garramone; p. 214: Photo © Brian VandenBrink, Photographer, 2003, Archi-tect: Ted Wengren, South Freeport, ME; p. 215: (top left) Photo © Brian VandenBrink, Photographer, 2003, Architect: John Martin, Torrington, CT; (top right) Photo © davidduncanliv-ingston.com; (bottom right) Photo © Brian VandenBrink, Photographer, 2003, Architect: Lo Yi Chan, New York, NY; p. 216: (top right) Photo © Brian VandenBrink, Photographer, 2003, Architect: Mark Hutker & Associates, Vineyard Haven, MA; (bottom left) Photo Charles Miller © The Taunton Press, Inc.; p. 217: (top and bot-tom) Photo Kevin Ireton, © Taunton Press, Architect: Geoff Prentiss, Seattle, WA; p. 218

(top left) Photo © Brian Vanden Brink; Design: South Mountain Builders, West Tisbury, MA; (top right) Photo © 2003 carolynbates.com, Architect: Brad Rabinowitz, Burlington, VT; (bottom): Photo by Andy Engel © The Taunton Press, Inc.; Architects: Brad Rabinowitz and Don Welch, Burlington, VT; p. 219 (top right) Photo © davidduncanlivingston.com; (bottom left) Photo © Brian VandenBrink, Photographer 2003, Architect: Weston Hewitson Architects, Hingham, MA; p. 220 (top) Photo © Jessie Walker; (bottom) Photo © James Westphalen; p. 221 (bottom left) Photo © davidduncanlivingston.com; (bottom right) Photo © Brian VandenBrink, Photographer 2003, Architect: Lo Yi Chan, New York, NY; p.222 (top left) Photo © davidduncanlivingston.com; (bottom right) Photo © Brian VandenBrink, Photogapher 2003, Architect: Tom Catalano, Boston, MA p. 223 (top) Photo by Charles Miller © The Taunton Press, Inc; Architect: Robert Orr & Assoc. LLC, New Haven, CT; (bottom) Photo by Charles Bickford © The Taunton Press, Inc., Architect: David Sellers, Warren, VT; p. 224 (top:) Photo © Jessie Walker, Design: Greene & Proppe Designs, Chicago, IL; (bottom) Photo by Charles Miller © The Taunton Press, Inc.; p. 225 (top) Photo © Jessie Walker, Design: Cynthia Muni, Northfield Ctr., OH; (bottom) Photo © 2003 carolynbates.com, Architect: J. Graham Goldsmith Architects, Burlington, VT; p. 226 (top)

Photo by Charles Miller, Design: Bobby Cucullo and Paul Duncker, Wilson, WY; (bottom) Photo © Jessie Walker, Design: Dave Hagerman, Hagerman Kitchens, Lansing, MI; p. 227 (top) Photo © Jessie Walker, Architect: Mastro-Sklar Architects, Chicago, IL; (bottom) Photo by Charles Miller © The Taunton Press, Inc., Designer: Jim Garramone, Evanston, IL; p. 228 (top) Photo © 2003 carolynbates.com, Architect Brad Rabinowitz, Burlington, VT; (bottom left) Photo by Charles Miller, © The Taunton Press, Inc., Architect: Ann Finnerty, Boston, MA; (bottom right) Photo ©Mark Samu, courtesy Hearst Specials; p. 229 (top and bottom) Photos © Jessie Walker; p. 230 (top left) Photo © Mark Samu, Architect James DeLuca, AIA, Huntington, NY; (bottom) Photo by Charles Miller © The Taunton Press, Inc., Designer: Jim Garramone, Evanston, IL; p. 231 (left) Photo© Jessie Walker, Designer: Blair Baby, Wilmette, IL; (right) Photo ©davidduncanlivingston.com; p. 232 Photo © davidduncanlivingston.com; p. 233 (top left) Photo © www.bobperron.com, Architect Paul Bailey, New Haven, CT; (bottom left) Photo © Mark Samu, Builders: John Hummel Construction, East Hampton, NY; (right) Photo © Ken Gutmaker; p. 234 (top) Photo © Mark Samu, courtesy Hearst Specials; (bottom) Photo by Roe Osborn © The Taunton Press, Inc., Architect: Damian Baumhover, San Diego, CA; p. 235 Photo © Jessie Walker; (bottom) Photo © Ken Gutmaker; p. 236 (left) Photo ©

2003 carolynbates.com, Designer and general contractor: Dana Ennis, Ennis Construction Inc., Ascutney, VT.; (top right) Photo © Brian VandenBrink, Photographer, 2003; Interior Design: Jane Langmuir Interior Design, Providence, RI; p. 237 (top) Photo © 2003 Rob Karosis/www.robkarosis.com; (bottom) Photo by Tom O'Brien ©The Taunton Press, Inc.; p. 238: (top) Photo courtesy Wallcandy Arts, www.wallcandyarts.com; (bottom) Photo © www.steve-vierra-photography.com; p. 239: Photo by Charles Miller, © The Taunton Press, Inc.; p. 240: Photo © 2005 Carolyn L. Bates/www.carolynbates.-com; p. 241: (top & bottom right) Photo © 2005 Carolyn L.Bates/www.carolynbates.-com; (bottom left) Photo © Robert Perron; p. 242: (top) Photo © GetDecorating.com; (bottom) Photo © Scott Zimmerman; p. 243: (top) Photo © Wendell T. Webber; (bottom) Photo © Tim Street-Porter; p. 244: Photos © Wendell T. Webber; p. 245: (top) Photo © Wendell T. Webber; (bottom) Photo courtesy Pi Smith, Smith & Vansant Architects, Norwich, VT; p. 246: (top) © Sargent 2002; Marc-Michaels Interior Design, Winter Park, FL; (bottom left) © Ken Gutmaker; (bottom right) Photo courtesy Charles Wilkins; p. 247: Photo courtesy York Wallcoverings; p. 248: (left) © Anice Hoachlander/Hoachlander Davis Photography; Barnes Vanze Architects, Washington, D.C.; (right) ©

Tria Giovan; p. 249: (top) © Steve Vierra Photography (bottom) © John Rapetti; The Office of Carol J.W. Kurth, AIA, Architects; p. 250: James Levine Photography, courtesy www.wallcandyarts.com; p. 251: (top) Photo courtesy Wallies; (bottom left) © 2002 Douglas A. Salin, www.dougsalin.com; Sherry Scott, ASID, CID, Design Lab, Redwood City, CA; (bottom right) © Michael Lyon; Hayslip Design Associates, Dallas, TX; p. 252: (top) Photo courtesy Velux-America Inc.; (bottom) © Andrea Rugg Photography; Christine L. Albertsson AIA, Albertsson Hansen Architecture, Ltd., Minneapolis, MN; p. 254: (top) Photo courtesy Pi Smith; Smith & Vansant Architects, Norwich, VT; (bottom) © Philip Beaurline; p. 255: (top left) © Mark Samu, Samu Studios Inc.; (top right) Kate Coffey; Smith & Vansant Architects, Norwich, VT; (bottom) Courtesy York Wallcoverings; p. 256: © Graham Architects; Jeffrey O. Graham, AIA, Graham Architects, San Francisco, CA; p. 257: (top) © Thomas Sconyers, Photom Studios; Patricia Davis Brown, CKD, CBD, Patricia Davis Brown Fine Cabinetry, Vero Beach, FL; (bottom) © Anne Gummerson Photography; p. 258: (top) Photo © Chipper Hatter; (bottom left) Photo © Scott Zimmerman; (bottom right) Photo © www.davidduncan-livingston.com; p. 259: Photo © Eric Piasecki; p. 260: Photos © Olson Photographic, LLC; Designs by Lisa Newman Interiors, Barrington, RI; p. 261:

Photos © Lisa Romerein; p. 262: (top left) Photo courtesy Posh Tots; (top right) Photo © Mark Samu; Design by Lee Najman Design; (bottom) Photo © Greg Premru; p. 263: (top) Photo © www.davidduncanlivingston.com; (bottom) Photo © Robert Perron; p. 264 (left) Photo © Ken Gutmaker; (right) Photo © Brian VandenBrink, Photographer, 2003, Architect: George Suddell, Westbury, NY; p. 265 (top) Photo © www.bobperron.com, Architect: Burr & McCallum, Williamstown, MA; (bottom right) Photo © Brian Vanden-Brink, Photographer, 2003, Archi-tect: Bernhard & Priestly Architects, Rockport, ME; p. 266 (top) Photo © www.-bobperron.com, Designer: Diane Yohe, Norwalk, CT; (bottom) Photo © davidduncanliv-ingston.com; p. 267 Photo © 2003 carolynbates.com, Designer: Donna L. Sheppard, Sheppard Custom Homes, Colchester, VT; p. 268 (top) Photo © Brian VandenBrink, Photographer, 2003; Architect: Centerbrook Architects, Essex, CT; (bottom) Photo © James R. Salomon Photogra-phy, Design: Orcutt Associates, Yarmouth, ME; p. 269 (left) Photo ©davidduncanliving-ston.com; (right) Photo © Ken Gutmaker; p. 270 (top) Photo © 2003 carolynbates.com, Builder: Erich C. Gutbier, Arlington, VT; (bottom) Photo © James R. Salomon Photogra-phy; Design: Orcutt Associates, Yarmouth, ME; p. 271 Photo © davidduncanlivingston.com p. 272 Photo © Brian Vanden-Brink, Photo-grapher, 2003,

Builders: Axel Berg Builders, Falmouth, ME;p. 273 (top and bottom) Photos © Brian VandenBrink, Photographer, 2003; Design: Custom Electronics, Falmouth, ME; p. 274 Photos © Brian VandenBrink, Photographer, 2003, Design: Custom Electronics, Falmouth, ME p. 275 Photo © Mark Samu, Design: Langsam Rubin Design, Oyster Bay, NY; p. 276 Photo © www.bobperron.com, Architect: David Goetsch, Stamford CT; p. 277 (top) Photo © Mark Samu, courtesy Hearst Specials; (bottom) Photo © 2003 carolynbates.com, Interior design: Nancy Heaslip; p. 278: (top) Photo © 2005 Carolyn L. Bates/www.car-olynbates.com; (bottom left) Photo courtesy Levels of Discovery; (bottom right) Photo © Wendell T. Webber; p. 279: Photo by Randy O'Rourke, © The Taunton Press, Inc.; p. 280: Photo © Rob Karosis; p. 281: (top) Photo © Wendell T. Webber; (bottom) Todd Caverly, photographer © 2005; G.M. Wild Construction, Brunswick, Maine.; p. 282 (top left) Photo © Brian VandenBrink, Photographer, 2003, (bottom left) Photo © www.carolynbates.com, Designer: Pat Pritchett, Vermont Vernacular Design, South Woodbury, VT; (top right) Photo © James R. Salomon Photography, Architect: Salmon Falls Architects, Saco, ME; p. 283 (top) Photo © www.carolyn-bates.com, Architect: Malcolm Appleton, AIA, Interior design: Barbara Stratton, both from Waitsfield, VT; (bottom) Photo

© Jessie Walker, Designer: Dave McFadden, Geneva, IL; p. 284: Photo courtesy PoshTots, PoshTots.com; p. 285 (left): Photo courtesy La Petite Maison, lapetitemai-son.com; p. 286: Photo cour-tesy Katelynscastles; p. 287: (top left) © 2003 Keenan Ward; Robert Mahrer General Contractor Inc., Santa Cruz, CA; (top right) © 2003 Keenan Ward; Robert Mahrer General Contractor Inc., Santa Cruz, CA; (bottom) Photo courtesy Katelynscastles; p. 288: © Anderson-Moore Builders, Inc. Photos by Sharon Haege, Brick House Creative; Anderson-Moore Builders, Inc., Winston-Salem, NC; p. 289: (top) Photo courtesy La Petite Maison, lapetitemai-son.com; (bottom) © Robert Perron; p. 290: (left) Photo courtesy Mark IV Builders, Inc., Photo by Woody Cady Photography; (right) © Allyson Jones; Allyson Jones, Wall Art Studio, Altadena, CA, www.allysonjonesmurals.-com; p. 291: (top and bottom) © Andrea Rugg Photography; Christine L. Albertsson AIA, Albertsson Hansen Architec-ture, Ltd., Minneapolis, MN; p. 292: (left) © Randy Brown Architects.com; (right) Photo courtesy Timothy Rice, Assoc. AIA, on behalf of the American Heart Association, MN; p. 293: © 2003 Feinknopf Photography; Richard Taylor, AIA, Richard Taylor Architects, LLC, Dublin, OH; p. 294 (top) Photo © 2003 carolynbates.com, Architect: Malcolm Appleton, AIA, Waitsfield, VT; (bottom) Photo © Mary Gamache Schumer;

p. 295 (top) Photo © Brian VandenBrink, Photographer, 2003, Architect: Rob Whitten, Portland, ME; (bottom) Photo © Jessie Walker; p. 296 (top) Photo © Rob Karosis/ www.robkarosis.com, Builder/developer: The Green Company, Newton, MA; (bot-tom) Photo © Jessie Walker; p. 297 (top) Photo © Jessie Walker; bottom: Photo © 2003 carolynbates.com; Architect Brad Rabinowitz, Burlington, VT; p. 298 (top) Photo © Ken Gutmaker; (bottom) Photo © Robert Perron, Photographer, Architect: Robert W. Knight Architects, Blue Hill, ME; p. 299 Photo © Robert Perron, Photographer, Architect: Robert W. Knight Architects, Blue Hill, ME; p. 300 Photo © davidduncanlivingston.com; p. 301 (top) Photo © Brian VandenBrink, Photographer, 2003; (bottom) Photo © Jessie Walker; p. 302: © NAI Architecture/Planning/Interio rs; William K. Mayfield, AIA, NAI Architecture/Planning/ Interiors, Mount Hermon, CA; p. 303: Photo courtesy Thomas L. Chamberlain, AIA, San Jose, CA